KU-191-738

The kangaroo which stole a five pound note, the soldier who stowed his girlfriend in his kitbag, artificial icebergs, the penicillin black market in Berlin, the golden eagle which travelled in a laundry basket, how the Vatican was invaded by white ants, the elephant that water-skied, the couple who lived in a tree, the 101-year-old lady who slid down banisters, the curry which turned a girl pink... Add to that Lucky Luciano's funeral, the last days of Nijinsky, Casanova's autobiography, Picasso's painting machine, the curse of the Hope diamond and the founding of the Order of the Mosquito... and you have *Amazing Times!*

Also published by Unwin Paperbacks

THE FIRST CUCKOO
Letters to *The Times* 1900-1980
chosen and introduced by
Kenneth Gregory

Stephen Winkworth was educated at Winchester and Balliol College, Oxford. After working as a news reader for Vatican Radio, he joined Chapman & Hall, Evelyn Waugh's publishers, as a scientific and general books editor. He then worked for four years at the United Nations in Rome, drafting technical and policy reports. He is also an inventor of remote-control devices, including radio-controlled sharks, which patrol millionaires' beaches, and the first flying model of *Pteranodon Ingens*. He is the author of *Great Commercial Disasters* and *Famous Sporting Fiascos*. An article by him on *Pterodactyls and the British Economy* is currently being prepared for press. He is related to the Rev. C.L. Dodgson (Lewis Carroll) and the Rev. W.A. Spooner, who gave his name to Spoonerisms.

AMAZING
TIMES!

a selection of the most amusing and amazing articles from

1945–1981

chosen by
STEPHEN WINKWORTH

illustrated by
ffolkes

London
UNWIN PAPERBACKS
Boston   Sydney

First published in Great Britain by George Allen & Unwin 1982
First published in Unwin Paperbacks 1983
Reprinted 1983

This book is copyright under the Berne Convention.
No reproduction without permission. All rights reserved.

UNWIN ® PAPERBACKS
40 Museum Street, London WC1A 1LU

This edition and selection © Stephen Winkworth 1982
Illustrations © Michael ffolkes 1982

Copyright in the articles published in this volume
belongs to Times Newspapers Ltd except as specified
in the Acknowledgements on page 245 hereof.

ISBN 0 04 808039 X

Set in 11 on 12 point Plantin Light by Text of Orpington
and printed in Great Britain by Guernsey Press Co. Ltd.,
Guernsey, Channel Islands.

INTRODUCTION

News, as a rule, is far from astonishing – even when it is good. Occasionally, however, events are reported which support the view that the world is a funny place. It is suddenly discovered that half the universe is going backwards or that the Vatican has been invaded by ants. We are told that the city of Adelaide has miraculously escaped the threat of doomsday or that the Chinese are planning to breed a near-human monster. Such disclosures are the more startling when their source is factual and authoritative; for nothing is truly amazing, or funny, or even interesting, unless one can believe in it. Take, for instance, the information that the Bishop of Bath has no soap, or that a lady of 101 enjoys sliding down banisters. As examples of the comic imagination they would hardly be surprising, but when *The Times* reports that such things have actually happened they assume an altogether different complexion.

It is delightful to come across such reports because they reveal that life, far from being as humdrum as it so often seems, remains bizarre and unpredictable; but the enjoyment in reading them derives from their style as much as their content. Words are themselves a major preoccupation of *The Times*, and verbal curiosities and innovations are as much cause for comment as political events. The observation of words is valuable in maintaining the strength and purity of the language, but it is also entertaining, and word-watching has now become something of a national pastime – replacing the more magisterial function of linguistic pest control which *The Times* regarded as its appointed task in former days.

Besides the English language, the national character itself is reflected perhaps more clearly in *The Times* than in any other newspaper. It is said that the British are a phlegmatic race and that this can be readily observed from *The Times*, which makes a virtue of the low-key headline and the sober paragraph. I trust that this anthology will dispel any such notion for good, for I do not believe that any of the articles selected can conceivably be accused of excessive sobriety.

Of course, not every headline in a newspaper which aims at an unimpassioned chronicling of everyday events can sparkle with wit, no matter how brilliant the writer. Claud Cockburn's memoirs of his days in Printing House Square* give the impression of a coterie of eccentric mandarins, mostly Fellows of All Souls, translating Plato's *Phaedo* into Chinese and making improbable bets with each other. One of these bets was to devise the least sensational headline and to get it printed. Cockburn claims to have won the competition with SMALL EARTHQUAKE IN CHILE. NOT MANY DEAD. I have not been able to track down this item (presumably it appeared in the early thirties), but there have been many in a similar vein. The attitude of *The Times* to earthquakes during the first half of this century was certainly distinctive. In pre-electronic days ordinary news travelled more slowly, but seismographic events would reach the West Bromwich observatory instantly and readers of *The Times* would want to be informed of the slightest geological upheavals. While readers of lesser newspapers were only interested in spectacular damage, for the Stock Exchange and the City – *Times* readers to a man – all earthquakes were important, because they could affect financial interests. *The Times* was also, in a sense, a part of the apparatus which controlled the world, no corner of which could be allowed to quiver without its knowledge and supervision.

As new methods of news-gathering have made seismography less crucial, so other topics have come to the fore. Today's equivalents are the art market, the environment and the climate, whose fluctuations are watched with equal alertness. If Cockburn's competition were held today, the winners might be MINIATURES FAIL TO AROUSE MUCH INTEREST (December 1974), WORLD HAS WARMED BY 0·4°F SINCE 1965 (August 1981) or, as reported from Paris in 1970 (thanks presumably to a merciful scarcity of earthquakes), EIFFEL TOWER STANDING UP WELL.

Flushed with success at winning the competition, Cockburn went on to do something even more unforgivable. He

* *Cockburn Sums Up – An Autobiography* (Quartet, London, 1981).

devised a spoof report from Jerusalem based on an off-the-record interview with a certain Pontius Pilate about the 'Calvary Incident'. So *Times*-like was his report that the deception nearly worked. But at the last moment the Deputy Foreign Editor summoned him to his office and asked him in shocked tones whether he appreciated the gravity of attempting to play a joke on *The Times*.

I am confident that none of the items in this anthology is the product of a latter-day Cockburn. Many of them are too strange to have been invented. Others are notable for their revelation of amazing truths. There are, it seems, no limits to the things men and women will do to declare their love or hatred of each other. As for the revelations of science, they are as mind-boggling as the behaviour of scientists is grotesque. And what peculiar things happen when the paths of humans and animals cross!

The criteria used in compiling an anthology such as this cannot be defined in other than circular or negative terms. By 'circular' I mean that, as in a *Who's Who*, the contents define the book just as much as the book defines the contents. As for negative terms, there are no Law Reports, which is a pity since so many of them are extremely bizarre, but neither space nor sometimes the law itself allowed them to be included. There are no Bernard Levin articles, since he has himself collected them between hard covers. There is very little in the way of politics or crime. Politicians, like murderers, hardly ever depart from predictable patterns of behaviour, and when they do the results are too lamentable to be entertaining. There are no obituaries, because in many of the most interesting ones what is left tactfully unsaid is at least as astonishing as what is printed – and it would hardly be fair to relatives to write between the lines, or to readers not to. All the articles printed, however odd, are quite unretouched, beyond some standardization of spelling and punctuation, some occasional abridgement dictated by lack of space and the shortening of some of the longer headlines.

The process of finding these articles was like tramping through a vast forest in search of wild mushrooms. On every side impressive columns of information towered into the sky.

3

In certain parts of the forest – only a sixth sense can guide one to them – subtle influences combine to allow a single spore to germinate and burst through the flat soil into colourful fruition. But, as I soon began to appreciate, even where conditions seem ideal, there is no guarantee of making a find. The soil has to be just moist enough, the climate not too hot or too cold. August is not a good month – *The Times* grows drier in the 'silly season' – and January and February freeze out all but the hardiest varieties.

The discerning reader will not attempt to gulp down all the different species, with their wide variety of flavour and texture, together. Moreover, although every effort has been made to exclude *Cockburniensis deceptivus*, you will encounter one or two Death Caps and a handful of scarlet hallucinogens. Remember also the toadstool in *Alice in Wonderland*. One half turned Alice into a dwarf, the other made her tower over the earth like a giraffe. In these pages you will find both perspectives.

STEPHEN WINKWORTH

EARTHQUAKE SHOCK IN BRITAIN

One of the most disturbing earthquake shocks experienced in Britain for many years occurred early on Saturday morning, affecting a wide area, chiefly in the north of England.

Houses and other buildings more than 200 miles apart were shaken, but no damage was caused, and there were no casualties. In several Yorkshire towns and cities people were thrown out of bed, and large numbers, suspecting enemy activity, sought refuge in air-raid shelters. Earth tremors were felt in districts as widely separated as Carlisle and Cromer.

Proof of the time at which the disturbance occurred, as well as its violence, was provided at Stonyhurst, Lancashire, where the observatory instrument was put out of action at 1.35 a.m. The Kew seismograph recorded it at 36½ minutes past one. The tremor lasted about three minutes.

Mr. J. J. Shaw, the seismologist, of West Bromwich, traced the centre of the disturbance to an area somewhere between Manchester and Darlington. It was felt severely in Manchester, where even the most substantially built structures were shaken from top to bottom.

1 January 1945

[J. J. Shaw was responsible for many seismological reports in *The Times*. Starting as an amateur who built his own machines, Shaw eventually became recognized as an expert, and with Professor Milne designed the Shaw-Milne seismograph. His observatory in West Bromwich became one of the foremost in the country. He was awarded a CBE, and on his death in 1948 at the age of 74 his work received further acknowledgement in a Times obituary. Owing to current limitations in the art, his reports were sometimes disturbingly uncertain. An earthquake recorded by Mr Shaw on 28 June 1945, for instance, is reported as being 'about 6,000 miles away, probably in the west of the East Indies, or in the central Andes'.]

VICTORY PLANS IN A BATHROOM

When a 'Mulberry' harbour exhibition was opened in Liverpool yesterday, Mr R. P. Biddle, newly appointed north-west regional port director, stated that the first trials of the model section of the harbour took place in the Prime Minister's bathroom in a liner while he was going to a conference in Canada.

8 May 1945
[VE – Victory in Europe – Day]

'THIS WAR HAS BEEN MADNESS'
CROWN PRINCE'S VIEWS

LINDAU   The Crown Prince Wilhelm, eldest son of the late Kaiser, who was captured by French troops at his hunting lodge in Mittelburg, is now lodged at Lindau.

In a statement to a press representative yesterday he said: 'The German people have behaved like idiots. First they followed Ebert, then Hindenburg, then Hitler. This war has been madness. I always told papa before 1914 that we ought to have an understanding with France, but fathers don't like taking advice from their sons.'

Hitler, the Crown Prince said, dealt with everything himself and surrounded himself with second-raters. 'He was like a pretty woman who surrounds herself with ugly women.'

He had incredible power over the German crowds, but he was a failure as an international psychologist.

'Hitler understood neither the French nor the British mind,' the Crown Prince continued. 'I saw him two or three times and each time I told him he was making a mistake. I especially warned him about persecuting Catholics and Jews, but Hitler really hated the Jews.'

The Crown Prince declared that Mussolini was a brilliant man, but he lacked the material and the men to carry out a grand policy. His greatest error was the Ethiopian war.

12 May 1945

6

THE FOURTH AT ETON

War-time 'Fourths' have been, perhaps paradoxically, re-markable for their peaceful character. If only there had been no war they would have been perfect but that was a very big 'if'. The suspensory condition having now been removed, Saturday's festival was for many people as near perfect as might be.

The weather, so long legally unmentionable, appeared likely to be so in another sense, but after one fierce, early shower it relented and the day was one of fresh, breezy sunshine. Whether it was peace or the basic ration, the array of cars in Agar's Plough did the heart good to see, and there were quite enough people to make the hunting for any given person an exhausting and sometimes a vain quest. Everything seemed delightfully immutable save for one innovation, the mother who smoked a cigarette at Speeches. No lightning came down from heaven to consume her, yet it is to be hoped that this will not be taken as a precedent in Upper School.

That incident had an added piquancy for those who sat near, from one of the scenes in the Speeches themselves, the 'Row in the Pit', from Anstey's 'Voces Populi', in which the lady in the front row refuses to remove her hat, until it is suggested that she cannot do so without disaster. It was quite good fun, and so was, as indeed it cannot fail to be, the trial scene from 'Pickwick', though the necessary shortening of the evidence of Mr Winkle and Mrs Cluppins robbed it inevitably of some of its point. This was, however, one of the days on which the set pieces (to use the language of the still absent fireworks) came decidedly second to the single speeches. Several of them were capital. Burrows, KS, got the very best out of Stephen Leacock's account of that trinity of mathematical persons, A. B. and C, who are forever running races against one another at paces so diverse as to outrage all athletic probability.

Eddis was admirably quiet, and therefore impressive, in a passage from the Inquisition speech in Bernard Shaw's 'St Joan', and Ramsay was as appropriately vigorous in 'Holy Willie's Prayer'. His Scotch accent was, at any rate to an English audience, perfect, and he conveyed, very slyly and

with thanks to H M Bateman

'The mother who smoked a cigarette at Speeches . . .'
[THE FOURTH AT ETON]

pleasantly, the effect of denouncing the Provost and Vice-Provost who sat defenceless before him. Finally, Armstrong, KS, coming last but one, in the traditional position for the Captain of the School, gave de Quincey's account of the mail coaches driving laurelled out of London on the night of some Peninsular victory, at once an anticipation and an echo of VE Day which sent everybody away to lunch, agreeably early and in the best of tempers.

The cricket in Agar's Plough, where the band played, was a triumph for crabbed age rather than youth. The School, for whom Lutyens built up, if the verb be permissible, a sound innings of over 50, were doing very well until the perennial Cartwright, choosing the psychological moment to put himself on, induced three batsmen to give catches with rather mild strokes. Then when the Ramblers went in the but slightly less venerable Twining played a polished and masterly innings full of the latest of late cuts that was a joy to see. One who was captain of the eleven in 1909 has surely earned the right to lean on his bat for a moment after a short run, but Twining needed no such indulgence. It was sad that he did not quite get his hundred, and G. O. Allen, after some strokes of a highly seductive quality, departed too soon, but the Ramblers succeeded in winning by six wickets (it was a 12-a-side match) with a bare two minutes to spare.

Before that most people had gone to Fellows' Eyot to see the procession of boats, which displayed something more than traces of its old splendours. The crews of the Upper Boats wore the traditional costume save only for the hats, and the coxswains went one better and were cocked-hatted as of yore. In the Lower Boats the captains were in orthodox attire and the rest wore at least the appropriate ties with white shirts. One boat, which may be nameless, swamped, but there were no casualties.

4 June 1945

[The owners of private cars had recently been allowed, for the first time since the war, to buy petrol for 'pleasure and sport'.]

JAPANESE 'DEATH RAY'

NEW YORK   Japanese scientists invented a 'death ray', but after five and a half years' work, according to allied headquarters in Japan, the best they could do with it was to kill a rabbit at 40 yards. All that it did to humans was to leave them dizzy and tired for 12 to 24 hours. Still hopeful, the Japanese Government as recently as last spring appropriated 1,000,000 yen to enable them to continue development of the ray, which is described as the focusing of extremely short wireless waves into a beam.

8 October 1945

KANGAROO WITH £5 NOTE

SYDNEY   Somewhere in the Grafton hills there is a kangaroo wearing a man's waistcoat with a £5 note in one of the pockets.

Two days ago Mr William Thompson, a Grafton farmer, found the kangaroo caught in the wire fence of his property. Acting on an impulse, he removed his old waistcoat and put it firmly on the kangaroo. He then released the kangaroo, which bounded away, wearing the waistcoat. About three hours later Mr Thompson remembered with horror that there was a £5 note in one of the pockets of the waistcoat. Ever since then he and his friends have been scouring the countryside for the kangaroo, but so far without success.

2 November 1945

GIRL IN SAILOR'S KITBAG

An 18-year-old girl was found in a sailor's kitbag at Herne Bay railway station yesterday. At Ramsgate she and the sailor were seen talking on the platform after the sailor had taken a ticket for Margate and had put some of his luggage in the guard's van. As the girl was not seen either to enter the train or leave the station, railway officials telephoned the police at Herne Bay,

'. . . wearing a man's waistcoat'
[KANGAROO WITH A £5 NOTE]

11

where police entered the carriage in which the sailor was seated and made him unlock the kitbag. The girl stepped out. Both stated at first that they had not enough money to pay the girl's fare, but later they produced sufficient to pay for a ticket to London and were allowed to proceed.

10 January 1946

FLOATING AIR STATIONS OF ICE

Details were released last night of a project, never actually brought to fruit, which was mooted in 1942 for the provision of floating air stations which should be unsinkable and practically indestructible.

The originator was Mr Geoffrey Pyke, Director of Programmes at the Combined Operations headquarters, who, having noted the great difficulty of breaking up icebergs or ice-jams with explosives, conceived the idea of using a floating air landing strip made of ice, either for the provision of air escort for convoys in mid-Atlantic, or in connexion with an allied landing in Europe.

After investigation it was proposed to construct an artificial iceberg, of a mixture of ice and wood-pulp, in the shape of a ship 2,000 ft long, 300 ft beam, and displacing some 2,000,000 tons, self-propelled, and preserved from melting by refrigeration. Her complement was to be some 3,600 officers and men.

Some preliminary work was done in 1942–43 in Canada, where there is no lack of ice, but by then the lack of air escort in the Atlantic had been made good successfully by other means, and, as it appeared that invasion plans would not call for the use of icebergs, the project was abandoned.

1 March 1946

MORE ELASTIC TO BE USED

From 1 April elastic can be used without restriction in the manufacture of underwear, nightwear, outerwear, hose, shirt armlets, identification bracelets, pocket books, pram covers, umbrellas, pocket wallets, belts for outerwear, sanitary belts, attaché cases, suit cases, handbags, men's garters and suspenders, laces for any apparel or footwear, and curtains. Utility braces with elastic inserts or with elastic cord ends can also be manufactured for the home market from the same date.

27 March 1946

IMITATION PENICILLIN IN BERLIN

BERLIN   German police, in cooperation with British and American detectives, on Friday arrested seven men and three women here as members of a gang who since the beginning of the year have been manufacturing imitation penicillin, which on the black market has been fetching as much as £375 an ampoule.

The imitation takes two forms, one based on dextrose and the other on yellow face powder. There is a great illicit demand for penicillin here for the treatment of venereal disease. Supplies are strictly controlled by the British and American authorities, being reserved primarily for the treatment of their soldiers, and secondarily for the treatment of German women likely to spread disease. Otherwise supplies are not available.

22 April 1946

NEWS IN BRIEF

Mrs Emily Polhill, who lives near a prisoner of war camp at Walderslade, Chatham, was fined £1 at Chatham yesterday for throwing a piece of cake over the camp fence to one of the prisoners. The prisoner to whom she gave the cake was stated to have been sentenced to 28 days' detention with hard labour.

7 May 1946

[Earlier in the month a Catholic encyclical deploring

13

cruelty to prisoners of war had been withdrawn from the US zone at the request of the military authorities.]

OPERATION MOUSE

A Bridlington nurse on duty at Scarborough Hospital saw a mouse running about the ward. She could find no method of catching it so obtained an ethyl-chloride spray, drove the mouse into a corner, and sprayed the floor on both sides of it. The mouse ran into the spray and was anaesthetized, whereupon the nurse got a pair of forceps and removed it to be drowned.

3 June 1946

NIJINSKY'S LIFE IN VIENNA

VIENNA   One great figure of the stage has left and another has arrived in Vienna.

Nijinsky, who has been living in Sacher's Hotel for the last year, has gone to a country house near Salzburg with his wife. He came to Austria from Hungary at the end of the war, and was the only civilian living in Sacher's Hotel, which was requisitioned by the British, who gave him rations. He was in bad health, and remained mostly in his room, though sometimes he and his wife might be seen together in the streets or in the country. Some time ago his wife told correspondents that he had heard Russian music outside a window in the country, and had begun to dance, but it is impossible, except for a miracle, that he should ever dance seriously again. Nijinsky is now elderly in appearance, bald, and still immensely strong.

Recently there returned a great Viennese jester, Karl Farkas, who, with his partner Fritz Grunbaum, used to make the city laugh before the days of the *Anschluss* with their jokes and rhymes, often set to their own music. Both were Jews and made fun of the Nazis. Farkas escaped on the night of the *Anschluss*, but Grunbaum was caught and sent to Dachau, where he died. A big theatre was taken to welcome Farkas home, and an official reception was given him. Dr Victor Matekja, State Secretary for Fine Arts, who was also in Dachau, described how Grunbaum had given revues there, and how the Germans had ordered him to make jokes, threatening him with shooting if they were not good jokes. When he was dying Grunbaum gave Dr Matekja a message for his former partner, Farkas, telling him to 'return to Vienna and make the people laugh again'. Farkas said he had come for this purpose, and, though the audience were near tears, after a few minutes he had fulfilled it.

5 August 1946

FREEDOM FOR GOLDEN EAGLE

Tomorrow morning Keeper Hubert Jones, of the London Zoological Gardens, will leave Euston for Inverness, with a golden eagle in a laundry basket. The eagle was caught in a trap on a Scottish estate and was sent to the Zoological Gardens to have its injuries treated. It is now fit again and will be taken back to the spot where it was caught to be released. The eagle will travel at the parcels rate of 10s in a luggage compartment.

5 September 1946

CHARMS OF THE AUTUMN MIGRATION

It is one of the charms of the autumn migration that it brings within reach of the town or suburban naturalist at sewage farm or reservoir birds such as ruffs and reeves, greenshank, or little stints, which he might otherwise never have the good fortune to see. There is often, too, the opportunity for leisurely observation.

Here today and gone tomorrow is unfortunately the rule with birds of passage in the spring, but on the return journey they are in no hurry, and, finding a spot to their liking, will linger there for days. The 'spot' is often a sewage farm, which to the uninitiated may not seem the sort of place at which from choice to spend one's free time at week-ends, yet with the wind in the right quarter it is, for the bird-watcher who cannot get out into the 'real' country, an oasis of absorbing interest conveniently near at hand. This I know, having as a one-time townsman, spent so many Saturday afternoons at the local sewage farm, gazing over the low trimmed hedge at the snipe dibbling in the marshy runnels, often in large numbers, which in September were the very least one could expect.

There was almost always 'something else' to reward one's vigil – a green sandpiper, its white rump making the rest of its upper parts seem black as it rose from time to time in twisting flight; the ruffs (or were they reeves?) which unfortunately were not in breeding regalia but as easily watched as if they were in the Waders' Aviary at the Zoo; the little stints which also were absurdly tame. This year, in the first week of September, a sewage farm near Manchester was honoured by the presence of 'the rarer Temminck's stint'. It was with some little stints, and Mr P. Newton (who writes about it to *The Times*) was able, after many visits, to get within five yards and carefully compare the differences in plumage which make Temminck's stint appear a common sandpiper in miniature, the little stint a tiny dunlin. In voice and flight the rarer bird was also quite distinct.

20 September 1946

TRIBUTE TO 'WARRIOR BIRDS'

A memorial to 'warrior birds who gave their lives on active service, 1939–1945' was unveiled in the garden of All Hallows-by-the-Tower yesterday, the festival of St Francis of Assisi. Funds for the memorial had been collected by Miss Nancy Price.

The memorial consists of a small rowan tree trunk with forked branches set in a rough stone base which forms two pools for water: between the branches at different heights are wooden troughs for crumbs or other public offerings, and on the branches are birds carved in wood: pigeons, canaries, and sparrows.

16

The Rev. P. B. Clayton, vicar of All Hallows, conducted a short service of dedication. Miss Price, who explained that the rowan tree from which the memorial was made was from her own garden, said that on one war operation 27,000 pigeons were engaged – 17,000 in the actual operation – and less than 10 per cent survived, but those that did return brought back information of great value. Among pigeons with distinguished war records were 'Beachcomber', which came back from the Dieppe raid across 27 miles of sea in 32 minutes, and the 'Bey of Tunis', which carried the first report of the fall of Tunis to Eighth Army headquarters in a blinding rainstorm.

5 October 1946

NO SOAP FOR THE BISHOP

The Deputy Mayor of Bath (Mr Edgar Clements), speaking at the City of Bath Girls' School yesterday, said that when the Bishop of Bath and Wells, Dr H. W. Bradfield, first went to his Palace at Wells there was not one bar of soap in it. He applied to the right Government Department in London and received the reply: It is much to be regretted that saponaceous material cannot be found in the Palace, but we would suggest that other detergents may be available.'

21 November 1946

SOVIET WRITER'S TALE OF A DOG TSAR

MOSCOW   A State official, writing in the organ of the propaganda administration of the Communist central committee, calls for the protection for Soviet children from 'the morality of the zoo', found in a recent tale by the popular writer for children, Kornei Chukovsky.

The tale describes how a number of ill-treated dogs formed a band under a Tsar 'who wore a golden crown and lived in a golden kennel', and then seized and turned the tables on their masters, whom they fed on putrid food and kept on chains

'. . . the morality of the zoo'
[SOVIET WRITER'S TALE OF A DOG TSAR]

until they had learned to respect the morality of dogs. Then, wise, cultured, and kind, they were allowed to go home. In their realm, according to this tale, the dogs read newspapers, carried umbrellas, listened to the wireless, and bought and sold. The writer suggests that the publisher of this story was short-sighted.

14 December 1946

THE SPANIARDS' WORD FOR IT

Members of the Spanish Academy of the Language recently discussed throughout an entire session whether the word *extraperio*, the accepted term for the black market, should be admitted into the dictionary. They decided that it should not.

8 January 1947

BANANAS FLOWN TO SICK POET

NEW YORK   At 10.15 a.m. yesterday Mayor O'Dwyer, of New York, received a telegram from Mr John McCann, Lord Mayor of Dublin, which read as follows: 'Poet Eoghan Roe Ward dying. Bananas may save life. Is it possible send some by air?' Five hours later two hands of bananas were on their way to Rineanna airport – bought in New York and sent to La Guardia field in a police car in time to catch a Pan-American World Airways aeroplane. But prompt as Mr O'Dwyer was, the American Overseas Airline, though he did not know it, was prompter still. Already at 11 a.m., responding to an appeal from its Shannon office, it had dispatched four bunches of bananas to Eire.

20 January 1947

RURAL DEAN'S SURPLICE ON FIRE

Clothing worn by the rural dean of Bletchley, the Rev. C. A.

Wheeler, caught fire during a clergymen's service in Leighton Buzzard parish church yesterday. The back of the surplice was set alight by a candle while a hymn which referred to 'the consuming flames of sin' was being sung. The flames enveloped the back of the surplice without the rural dean noticing it. The vicar of Leighton Buzzard, the Rev. S. J. Forrest, stopped the service, rushed to his assistance and beat out the fire with his hands. Mr Wheeler's surplice and overcoat were burned but he was unhurt.

5 March 1947

CROSSWORDS IN THE CIVIL SERVICE

Colonel Frank Byers, Chief Liberal Whip, speaking at Luton last evening, said a complete overhaul of the Civil Service was long overdue. He quoted a letter from an architect in a Government office who had recently resigned. Among his reasons were the following:

Men earning high salaries spent hours and even days of working time in reading newspapers and doing crossword puzzles and private work. They habitually arrived half an hour late, left half an hour early, and took an hour and three-quarters for lunch. Work was not harmed, because there was seldom work to do. The staff was kept at an unduly large figure, and the writer added that the work for which he was engaged at a high salary showed no signs of materializing. Realizing that he was becoming incapable of working normally, he decided to resign. Colonel Byers said he did not suggest that this was typical of many Government offices, for many Civil Servants were excellent, but the fact that it could exist in certain departments showed the need for a complete review of the system.

19 April 1947

BOMBING BY BALLOON ACROSS PACIFIC

TOKYO   A detailed picture of one of the most novel experiments of the war in the Pacific has come to light by the discovery by the United States 1st Cavalry Division in the isolated ravines of the Otsu Peninsula, in Idaragi Prefecture, about 125 miles north of Tokyo, of the sites from which the Japanese in 1944 launched thousands of bombing balloons loaded with high explosive against the United States.

The concrete structures, which, complete with hydrogen generating plants, inflating platforms, launching platforms, and other facilities, are among the most elaborate installations discovered in Japan, are scattered over hundreds of acres. Of particular interest are the enormous concrete emplacements on which balloons were filled through pipelines, and loaded with bundles of explosives fitted with timing devices for their automatic release. Barracks capable of housing thousands of men were constructed near the sites.

The balloons soared high above the clouds and were borne toward North America by the prevailing eastward gales of the upper regions. Many never reached the target and presumably were lost over the sea, but some crossed the Pacific and reached America, where they did slight damage. It is believed the Japanese abandoned this method of bombing some months before the surrender because, owing to allied security, they received no news of the results of their experiment. It appears that they constantly awaited reports of the mysterious bombing of some American city and, when they finally heard nothing, they abandoned the project on which they expended such great efforts.

12 May 1947

CUCKOO FALSETTO

At the end of January residents in the Northstead area of Scarborough were claiming to have heard the first cuckoo. But yesterday Mr Hezekiah Johnson, a corporation road-cleaner, said: 'I wait until a crowd gathers at the Northstead bus-stop and then I go into the park nearby and do the cuckoo. They all take it in.' He added: 'I used to do the nightingale when I had my teeth in.'

6 February 1948

21

ALLEGED MALINGERING AT BAD NENNDORF

HAMBURG   The general court-martial hearing the second of the Bad Nenndorf cases again went into secret session here today to examine the intelligence record of Count Buttlar-Brandenfels, who, in his evidence against Captain J. S. Smith, RAMC, the medical officer of the camp, attributed the loss of four toes to his treatment in a freezing punishment cell last winter while he was held for interrogation by the British intelligence service. He is still in custody.

Mr. G. O. Slade, KC, for the defence, opening with the question: 'Do you know that your intelligence file describes you as a liar of truly gargantuan proportions?', established that the witness had received nine consecutive visits from the medical officer after his arrival at Bad Nenndorf, during which he never complained in writing about the condition of his feet, and went on to accuse him of malingering.

'Would I malinger four of my toes off?' answered Buttlar-Brandenfels, who hotly refuted a suggestion that he had already malingered to get out of the German Army. He was never in the German Army, he said, and he denied that he had been a member of the *Gestapo*, by whom he alleged he was arrested in 1943. He then dismissed as ridiculous a statement by one of the Bad Nenndorf interrogators that, aroused from his sleep the day he left the camp, he began to say 'We *Gestapo* men . . . ,' when, realizing his mistake, he stopped short. He was, he explained, in a high fever that night.

The rest of the hearing on these points was held *in camera*.

13 April 1948

BANISTER-SLIDING AT 101
MISS DOLPH ENLIGHTENS 'THE TIMES'

DUNMORE (PENNSYLVANIA)   Miss Florence Dolph, who is 101 years old, is anxious to teach the Editor of *The Times* the fine points of banister-sliding.

The Times, in a leading article published on Friday, mused on how Miss Dolph spent her day after sliding down the

'. . . down the banisters to breakfast'
[BANISTER-SLIDING AT 101]

banisters to breakfast on her 101st birthday. 'We have no vestige of right to assume she spent the rest of the day in a rocking-chair,' the leading article said. 'Not at all,' Miss Dolph replied yesterday. After the slide she helped in the preparations for her usual birthday party. After lunch she exchanged reminiscences with friends and relatives, drank a cup of tea, and walked in her garden. Then she read the many messages of congratulation. 'There was no time for rocking-chair sitting,' Miss Dolph said.

The article suggested that instead of sitting in a rocking-chair Miss Dolph was far more likely to have been crouching over the controls of a helicopter. 'It's not such a bad idea,' Miss Dolph said. 'I think I'll look into it.'

The article also wondered whether she adopted the forward seat in banister-sliding or whether she slid astride or side-saddle. Miss Dolph laughed. She slides down the banisters like a man – astride, not side-saddle. 'Tell that Editor to come on over,' she said. 'I'll not only show him; I'll teach him.' Miss Dolph does not confine her slides to birthdays – she straddles the banisters on holidays too.

7 June 1948

HIGH HOPES IN ARCHERY

The state of archery in England is causing anxiety among members of the Grand National Archery Society, governing body of the sport. One problem is the 'lone archer'. Our island, it seems, contains many of these solitary enthusiasts – men and women who shoot in modest back gardens and pine for the company of fellow-archers without knowing that there are archery clubs up and down the country, and a grand national society eager to put lone archers in touch with each other and with the clubs.

The best of England's archers, 20 men and 20 women, will compete in the twelfth international archery tournament, to be held next month at Dulwich College. There are high hopes of our archers carrying off many of the prizes and possibly establishing world records, for our national skill in archery is sound if not widely diffused among the people. The grand national society has taken at least one orthodox step towards improving matters: it has appointed a public relations officer.

A short talk on archery was accordingly arranged at the Archers Hall of the Royal Toxophilite Society yesterday, when Mr Weston Martyr, the author, and an enthusiastic archer, explained some aspects of the sport. He has been greatly impressed with the keen interest that Americans take in archery and stated that there are many thousands of archers in the United States. He considers that Americans like archery mainly because it is difficult. They like also to study things thoroughly, and by this method they settled the question of whether an archer at Agincourt could have pierced the armour of a French nobleman with his arrow.

The Doubting Curator

It seems that they hired the appropriate armour from a museum in New York and stuffed it with liver, after having (only with difficulty) persuaded the doubting curator that it would be unsafe for him to get into the armour himself. They shot an arrow of the Agincourt type at a range of 60 yards. It went through the armour and the mail, sparks and liver sputtered out, and the far side of the armour was heavily dented by the arrow-head. The curator had fainted.

After that, no visitor should feel inclined to wander too close to the targets at Dulwich next month. The present authentic long-distance record for a 'flight shoot' is 608 yards, held by an American; there is some hope that it may be beaten at Dulwich. There is an ancient record of 907 yards, about which there is no written evidence but only marking posts (or columns) set up in Constantinople: it belongs to the distant days when the Turks, with their own curious type of bow, were the great archers of the world. They seem to have lost the art and will not be sending any competitors to Dulwich.

Mr Weston Martyr, who told us a great deal more about archery, left the story to others when he reached the period at which 'some ass invented gunpowder'.

20 July 1948

LORD WAVELL ON VIRGIL

Lord Wavell, in his presidential address to the Virgil Society yesterday, dealt largely with the *Aeneid* regarded from a military point of view.

His translations must be some of the freest made to the society. The bull's-eye which Ascanius scored on the boasting Numanus was recorded as a very special event deserving very special commendation. '*Macte nova virtute puer, sic itur ad astra*' Lord Wavell rendered freely as 'Attaboy, you for the next Olympic Games.' He also suggested a Press headline for the incidents of the Eighth Book – 'Venus Vamps Vulcan. Son gets Shield.'

Virgil's manoeuvres to avoid writing of battles displayed poetical generalship of a high order. Though Virgil was the most unmilitary person and obviously hated war one could almost compile a textbook of military maxims from his writings. There were such as *Tu ne cede malis, sed contra audentior ito quam tua te fortuna sinet; O passi graviora dabit deus his quoque finem: Una salus victis nullam sperare salutem*, and *Timeo Danaos et dona ferentes* – a counsel of prudence in dealing with cunning enemies which the Trojans would have done well to have construed as 'always look a gift horse in the tummy'.

Aeneas as General

He wondered whether Aeneas as a commander-in-chief was modelled on Julius Caesar; it would be natural that he should be. The pattern of Caesar's great battles against the Nervii and Vercingetorix bore some resemblance to the battle in Book IX of the *Aeneid*. In accord with the practices of Julius Caesar, Aeneas showed a good deal of care in his military moves. No dashing commander, he was the prudent, anxious head of a host of refugees who would rather achieve his purpose by diplomacy than fighting. Aeneas had a real care for his men, and there was a true feeling of that spirit of comradeship which was the one great gift of soldiering and war. That did not come to Virgil from the *Iliad*, but from a knowledge of Julius Caesar's close comradeship with his men.

Aeneas made an effective if rather pedestrian general. There was a lack of imagination and cunning about him – he was taken in by the Wooden Horse, and accepted the not very bright suggestion to put on Grecian armour and crests which resulted, as might have been foreseen, in their being attacked by their own side.

Virgil may have received some pointers on soldiering from his friend Horace, who fought in Pharsalia, but there were sketches and incidents that showed that Virgil understood the business of soldiering, though Nisus and Euryalus, whose exploits and friendship were so praised, were thoroughly undisciplined soldiers who deserved a court-martial, had they survived.

Incident with Dido

In explanation of Virgil's treatment of Aeneas over the incident with Dido, Lord Wavell said that we could not reasonably apply Victorian moral standards to what happened over 2,000 years ago; the Dido business had been a little over-emphasized against the hero. The unusual feature in the *Aeneid*, as in the *Iliad*, was that the same War Cabinet controlled the operations of both armies.

Lord Wavell was a little shocked at the poor provision made for distinguished soldiers in Virgil's underworld. They seemed to lead a very dreary non-existence. Virgil could, however, make even an official casualty list sound musical:

> *Dardanidae, quos ille omnis longo ordine cernens*
> *Inemuit, Clauumque, Medontaque, Thersilochumque*
> *Tres Antenoridas, Cererique Sacrum Polyboeten.*
> *Idaeumque etiam currus etiam arma tenentem.*

Virgil, even in his treatment of what was to him the distasteful subject of military matters, was a very great poet indeed.

14 October 1948

TAXIS FOR TRAMPS

The Essex County Council welfare committee has instructed its officers that tramps stranded late at night are to be given taxis to convey them to the nearest county council hostel or institution. During the daytime they will be given their bus fares to the nearest hostel. Where no welfare officer is available the tramps are to apply to the police for help.

18 October 1948

FINDING THE LENGTH OF A YARD

The committee recently appointed to review existing legislation on weights and measures went to the root of the matter yesterday and inspected the Imperial Standard Yard and the Imperial Standard Pound. On these two 'imperials', as they are almost affectionately called at the Standards Department of the Board of Trade, are based all the legal measures for Great Britain.

They are ordinarily inspected only once every 10 years, an occasion which is known as the decennial comparison of the standards; at the intervening quinquennial comparison of the standards only the five 'parliamentary copies' are inspected. One each of these copies is kept at the Houses of Parliament, the Royal Observatory, the Royal Society, the Royal Mint, and the Standards Department. They are permitted to vary from the 'imperial' by as much as one part in 100m.

To produce the 'imperials' for yesterday's occasion three men, the holders of three different sets of keys, had to assemble in a strong room to unlock the relevant safe. The Imperial Standard Yard, made of a kind of bronze called Bailey's metal, was then taken to another room and set on a table on some special rollers designed to keep it level. The length of the yard is the distance between two scratches on two gold plugs sunk into the bar of Bailey's metal.

Under Glass Tumbler

The Imperial Standard Pound is a cylindrical-shaped piece of platinum. It was covered with a glass tumbler while waiting on the table for the committee to arrive. Afterwards it was

28

wrapped in special paper, then put in a silver-gilt thimble, which was placed in a gun-metal cask, which was placed in the iron safe in the strong room.

The 14 members of the committee were impressed with what they saw. The occasion was not made unduly solemn and there was little to warn the committee of which table bore the 'imperials' beyond a red-lettered notice reading 'Please do not touch'. The idea that the tumbler was placed over the pound to keep the committee's breath off it was dispelled by the tumbler being occasionally raised.

The committee did not linger over the 'imperials' because there were many other things to see at the Standards Department. There was Cater's balance, which is sensitive to a grain (or 1/7,000th part of a pound) and had in one scale a 100-lb weight, which is the largest legal weight in our country. And there was the finest balance in the department, the scale of which is divided into 1/100ths of a grain and is sensitive to ·0000438 grain. They were impressive instruments, but the 'imperials' were the more precious sight.

1 December 1948

[The Committee would have done well to give a little more of their time to the 'imperials'. Ten years later, when the bronze yard was re-examined, it was found to be shrinking at a worrying one millionth of an inch per year.]

ELEPHANTINE TACT

COLOMBO   The behaviour of a female elephant has reunited a couple who quarrelled and separated within a few months of their marriage. A young man from a village near Nawalapitiya in Ceylon married a girl from another village about seven miles away. His wife took a great interest in Hurathali, his elephant, and every morning fed the animal with fruits, sugar candy, coconuts, or sugar cane. The elephant also became very fond of her mistress.

One day the wife returned to her parents' home, having quarrelled with her mother-in-law. After that the elephant refused to take food and would do no work. She appeared to be ill and heart-broken. One morning the animal was missing.

Approaching the young woman's home, Hurathali began trumpeting. On seeing her mistress, the elephant waved her trunk, went close to her, and caressed her with her trunk. The young woman was so touched by this behaviour of the elephant that she returned to her husband's home.

31 May 1949

BAUDELAIRE EXONERATED AFTER 92 YEARS

PARIS   The criminal court of the Court of Cassation today quashed the conviction of the poet Charles Baudelaire, who was fined in 1857 for an offence against public morals in publishing *Les Fleurs du Mal*, six poems from which were ordered to be suppressed. Under a law passed in 1946 revision of such convictions is now possible in certain circumstances.

1 June 1949

LAST OF THE CHIMNEY BOYS

Mr Joseph Lawrence, who lives with his son on Lady (Murrough) Wilson's estate at Windlesham, Surrey, celebrates his 104th birthday today. He is believed to be the oldest man in England.

Mr Lawrence was born at Henley-on-Thames. At eight years of age he began work as a paper delivery boy, and at 12 was apprenticed to a chimney sweep. Until the use of chimney boys was made illegal he worked sometimes 15 hours a day climbing the insides of chimneys and sweeping down the soot

'Joe scrambled aloft again . . .'
[LAST OF THE CHIMNEY BOYS]

with a handbrush. Once he was employed to explore the chimneys of a large house in which a boy had vanished, and found the missing lad asleep in a bend in the chimney. Another time Mr Lawrence came down the wrong shaft, and with only a coat of soot to hide his nakedness found himself in a woman's bedroom. As she was in bed there was a lot of shrieking before Joe scrambled aloft again.

For more than 40 years Mr Lawrence was employed as a gas worker at a private estate near Henley, and he lived at Henley for 82 years. He is the oldest Oddfellow in Britain, and the last surviving chimney boy.

16 June 1949

CASE OF HANNS JOHST

BERLIN   The decision of a denazification court in Munich to classify Hanns Johst as not more than a 'fellow-traveller' of the Hitler movement is sharply criticized here. Johst held high rank in the SS, the so-called dagger of honour: he was president of the Reich Chamber of Literature, a body which controlled authors, translators and publishers and excluded all who refused to toe the party line; and he was a friend of Himmler's. His play *Schlageter*, based on a martyr of the French occupation of the Ruhr after the war of 1914–18, contained the sentence, 'When I hear the word "culture" I cock my revolver.' Johst was ordered to pay in instalments a fine of 500 marks. The *Neue Zeitung*, the organ of the United States Military Government, today raises the question whether the judge of the court which heard Johst's case ought not himself to be arraigned.

9 July 1949

A MEAL PREPARED 5,000 YEARS AGO

CAIRO   An ancient Egyptian noblewoman's dinner, buried with her in her tomb at Saqqara 5,000 years ago and found by

Mr W. B. Emery in 1937, will be seen in Cairo Museum once the problem of transporting it from the storerooms at North Saqqara has been solved. It is so fragile that the slightest jar could destroy it, so light that the gentlest puff of wind would dissipate it in dust. Mr Emery filled the back of a motor-car with cushions and sat on them with the dinner in a special box resting on cushions on his knees, but after a few moments it became evident that the meal would not survive even the shortest part of the 20-mile drive to Cairo.

The dinner was of high standard. Clearly recognizable, though now completely desiccated, are vegetable soup, a small sole-like fish, pigeon stew, quails with their heads tucked under their wings, kidneys, ribs of beef, bread, cakes, fruit, and what might have been a sauce or kind of cornflour. Wine jars were not lacking. Two other dishes have not yet been identified. Archaeologists were puzzled when they noticed that some of the food was on alabaster plates and other on ordinary pottery; but Mrs Emery realized that the alabaster was for cold viands and the pottery for hot. The only un-answered question now is – in what order were the dishes eaten?

The noblewoman could not have enjoyed such a meal for many years before her death, for she could eat only on one side of her mouth and that with difficulty. Some kind of infection had paralysed one side of her jaw and the teeth were ossified and welded together with enamel. On the other side the teeth were worn down almost to stumps.

13 September 1949

PETS' OWN SERVICE

The animals went in two by two, and if a lion had been present it is possible that he would have lain down with the lamb who was at the pets' service at Holy Trinity Church, Hereford, this afternoon.

The service, attended by several thousand people, was organized by the vicar, the Rev. L. J. B. Snell, secretary of the Hereford branch of the RSPCA. Owners and their pets were

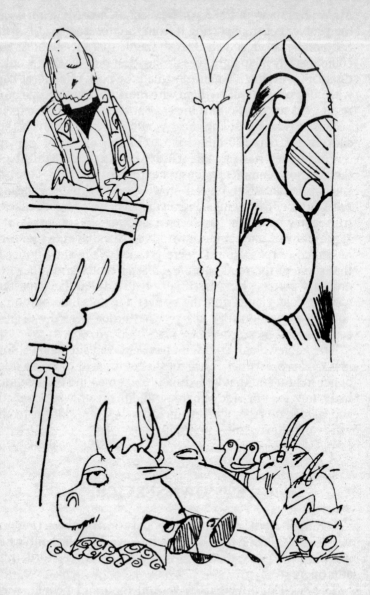

'The Dean of Hereford pronounced the blessing . . .'
[PETS' OWN SERVICE]

converging on the church in their hundreds for an hour before the service began, and the vicarage lawn looked like a menagerie.

The first arrival was a donkey, and among the many types of dogs present was a champion mastiff and her 10-week-old puppy. Pigeons, kittens, a duck on a dog's lead, a goat, and an 11-year-old tortoise were present, while a goldfish surveyed the scene from its bowl. The array of pets included also a Friesian calf and a Ryeland lamb and a dog, the inseparable companions of a small girl. Three other small girls who had no real pets came with their white toy dogs, and the whole procession was led to the church by the Rev. F. Dance on a brown horse. The animals lay quietly by their owners' sides as the Dean of Hereford, the Very Rev. H. R. Burrows, pronounced the blessing, the strange scene being disturbed only by the occasional clop of a horse's hoof on the church floor. Not a single fight was reported.

3 October 1949

VATICAN INVADED BY ANTS

ROME   An invasion of white ants in the Vatican has created anxiety about the safety of some of its valuable archives. The insects were first noticed about a week ago in the apartment of Cardinal Giovanni Mercati, librarian and archivist of the Holy Roman Church, which is situated in the Palace of the Zecca, and in the adjacent Courtyard of the Pappagalio, near which the archives of the Secretariat of State are kept.

The ants had been at their destructive work for some time in the Cardinal's apartment, where on Tuesday a beam across the ceiling of his bedroom cracked and threatened to collapse on to the Cardinal's bed. An inspection showed that most of the wood had already been eaten by ants, which, it was then discovered, had also invaded the other rooms of the apartment and attacked many of the books in the Cardinal's private library as well as furniture and clothing.

The walls of the buildings surrounding the Courtyard of the Pappagalio have now been carefully inspected foot by foot, and measures taken to destroy the nests of the ants as they are discovered, both there and in the apartment of Cardinal Mercati. It is understood that this prompt action has averted any immediate threat to the important archives of the Secretariat of State.

21 October 1949

VIGIL OF THE HOLY THORN

The holy thorns of Herefordshire, that open their flowering buds at midnight on Old Christmas Eve, have become one of the show pieces of western England. There is something sad about an ancient legend being dressed in modern garb, though it was admittedly comforting, in the cold midnight breezes on Orcop Hill, to be able to fortify oneself with 'hot dogs' and hotter tea from a motorized coffee stall, and to feel the unsolicited warmth radiated by arc lamps and captive Very lights that belong to the apparatus of Press photography.

About 1,000 people gathered round the holy thorn at Orcop last night. They had come by motor-coach from Hereford, Ross-on-Wye, Monmouth, and other towns; by car from Cardiff, Bristol, and still farther afield; and by bicycle and on foot from the neighbouring villages and countryside. The county police wisely arrived also, to deal with a traffic problem that was decidedly tricky.

Until the eve of Twelfth Night in 1948 the Orcop thorn had conformed to the Glastonbury legend, watched each year by no more than a score or so of local folk from farms and cottages. Then a Hereford newspaper published a letter about it, written by someone anxious to deny a statement that the famous holy thorn at Wormsley, uprooted by a gale in 1947, was the oldest in Herefordshire. As a result of that letter, the Orcop thorn was visited by several hundred people on the eve of Twelfth Night last year, and the crowd has grown still larger this year.

It was indeed mere curiosity that attracted nearly all the crowd to Orcop last night. There was little thought either for Joseph of Arimathea or the cold facts of botany. People were

36

concerned only to see whether or not the tree would blossom at the appointed hour of midnight. Yet, strangely enough, scarcely anyone was in the least concerned about the precise time. There was neither hush nor applause, nor any other concerted sign or recognition of midnight having arrived.

When Oxen Knelt

One old man of 70, a farm worker, has watched the Orcop thorn at the approach of Twelfth Night during most of the years of his life. He was there again last night, quite unconcerned about the great number of people now sharing his vigil without his own simple reverence. With the handle of his stick he would bend down a branch here and there, and shine his torch on the buds for any doubting watcher to see that they were coming out. Then he would explain that at midnight buds all over the tree would open. But the old man had not got a watch, and if he had had one it would have been no good setting it by the action of the buds he so fondly cherishes. He can look back, moreover, to the old days when, at the time that buds opened, oxen in the neighbouring fields knelt as if in veneration of what it signified.

There were not any oxen around last night, and if there had been they would probably have been scared by the flashlights, the innumerable torches and the general hubbub. Faith is not wholly absent from the make-up of England's people today, but most of those who watched the buds of the Orcop thorn opening last night heralded the sight with challenging matter-of-fact shouts. Others looked, but could not see things as their neighbours saw them.

The old man who has so often watched the Orcop thorn on Old Christmas Eve could at least take comfort in the fact that it had behaved better than the holy thorn a few miles away at Kingsthorne, which blossomed last week. Such deviations might ultimately upset his idea that the holy thorn is a last defence of the Old Style calendar, though he will probably forget all about that when he celebrates May Day in a few months' time on 13 May (OS).

7 January 1950

37

'FISHING' FOR TROUSERS

CAPETOWN   Among the sidelights on police work given by
Mr Swart, the Minister of Justice, to the House of Assembly
last night, was a warning to men against leaving their trousers
hanging over the backs of chairs, as there were thieves about
with hooks on long poles who stole such vulnerable trousers
through the windows. The Prime Minister himself, said Mr
Swart, left his trousers hanging over the chair in a hotel
bedroom. The door was not locked, and in the morning Dr
Malan found his trousers gone, together with his railway pass,
which was in a pocket.

Mr Swart also said that a woman in Johannesburg rang up
the police to report that a man in a tree was peering into her
room. A police van which had been called up by wireless
rushed to the scene, and the miscreant was caught – it turned
out to be a baboon, which was taken into custody and detained
in the zoo.

27 April 1950

THREAT TO A CZECH IN BELGIAN CONGO

LEOPOLDVILLE   The Czechoslovak Consul here said today
that he would protest against the 'expulsion' of a Czech
sculptor named Foit from the Belgian Congo. Mr Foit and his
wife were sent to South Africa last Saturday in a Belgian
military aircraft, 'for their own safety'. There had been riots in
Leopoldville during the day, and a mob of over 10,000
Africans threatened Mr Foit because they believed that he was
making night raids to kidnap them and turn them into 'corned
beef for export'. They seem to have mistaken some terracotta
models of the heads and bodies of Congolese, piled up in his
lorry, as the real thing. It is also said that some tinned foods
have appeared in the Congo with the head of a Negro as a trade
mark.

21 June 1950

CHANNEL SHIP CANARD

A three-word telegram sent from the British Railways cross-channel steamer *Brighton* yesterday gave rise to a rumour that the vessel had been involved in an accident. The telegram believed to have been sent to a relative of one of the passengers said 'Just struck mine'. Soon scores of inquiries were being made at Victoria and Waterloo. At 2.14 p.m. the *Brighton*, with about 500 passengers on board, docked safely at Dieppe. By then the rumour had gained hold on the French side of the Channel.

Later an official inquiry was made and a statement was issued by the Southern Region of British Railways confirming that two messages had been sent by a passenger from the steamer, one of which had given rise to a rumour that the ship had struck a mine. The messages, said the statement, were of a private nature, and when handed to the radio officer were dispatched in good faith. There was no truth in the rumour, and the ship was safe at Dieppe.

20 July 1950

MUSICAL 'FLYING SAUCERS'

ZERMATT   About a dozen persons living in the mountains above Basle have reported that on Thursday night they saw what they describe as 'flying saucers' which left a luminous wake in the sky. The saucers had a gyratory movement which they say was accompanied by a noise resembling organ music.

14 August 1950

'WAR' PANIC IN SWEDEN

STOCKHOLM   A little shamefaced, Swedes read in their newspapers today that people all over the country were misled by a 30-second radio 'stunt' last night. There was panic in some parts of the country when a mock announcement over the Swedish broadcasting system said that Swedish territory had been invaded by a western Power and that Sweden was likely to join the Russians in an imminent 'gigantic east–west clash'. Because of the announcement several ships in the Baltic Sea changed course and made for the nearest ports and Home Guard units turned out.

Thousands of people appear to have missed the explanation given half a minute later, that this had all happened in 1812 and that the invading forces were those of Napoleon I. Spokesmen of the State-owned broadcasting system today expressed their regrets that the effects of the broadcast had been 'far stronger than anticipated'.

29 September 1950

1895 CHEQUE IN LETTER-BOX

An unopened letter which was posted in Slough in 1895 and containing a cheque for £38 14s 4d, has been found by workmen in a letter-box during demolition of a house in Rocksborough Park, Harrow. The letter, addressed to a Mr W. F. Dauby, is believed to have been put into the box while it was freshly varnished and to have stuck to the back of it ever since. The cheque has been taken to the bank upon which it was drawn.

23 October 1950

'ATOMIC BOMB' SCARE IN NEW YORK

NEW YORK   Hundreds of persons in the Bronx borough of this city fled terrified from their houses into a subway station and other shelters last night on hearing a broadcast over a loudspeaker telling them to prepare for an atomic bomb attack – that unidentified aircraft were '30 – 20 – 10 miles' from the city, and finally 'all enemy aircraft have been encountered and destroyed'. Police traced the alarm to Stanley Gordon, a 23-year-old wireless amateur, who told them that he was merely testing his voice. He was sentenced to spend 30 days in the workhouse.

6 November 1950

CHILDREN'S GAMES ON TYNESIDE

Games played by children 50 years ago seem to have been fairly similar all over the country. An article on children's games in East London which appeared in *The Times* last Friday has prompted Mr F. Tait, of Dukeshouse Wood Camp School, Hexham, to write of games that were played in the streets of Gateshead, and Tyneside towns generally, at the beginning of the century.

In East London the boys used to play a straddling team game against a wall called 'Hi bobberee'. In Gateshead something similar was played called 'munt-a-cuddy'. As many as six boys would bend down in formation rather like a Rugby scrum, with the fattest boy standing upright as a buffer between the other boys and the wall. The second team would then leap on to the backs of the bending boys, the captain would shout 'Munt-a-cuddy! Munt-a-cuddy! One! Two! Three! Off! Off! Off!' and if his team managed to hang on it won.

A ring game similar to 'Here we go loopy loo', which was played in winter, was a summer game in the north:

> Hullabaloobie, loobie,
> Hullabalooba light,
> Hullabalooba, loobie,
> Upon a summer's night – oo!

Upon the exclamation everyone kicked the right leg in the air.

Seasonal Changes

Another ring game where two contestants tried to push each other out of the ring had a chorus:

> Gee's jaw, bull's snoot,

41

Vatty's in and skinny's oot.
Like a rotten, dotten dish cloot
Oot gaus he!

As in the south the games in the north were seasonal. While boys in London continued through the season to make their reins from coloured wool or string woven round tacks in the top of a cotton reel, in the north the boys would start this game, then would find the girls did it better than they and give it up as a game for girls only.

1 February 1951

DR HEWLETT JOHNSON ON THE BOAT RACE

A dispatch to *Pravda* on Dr Hewlett Johnson, the Dean of Canterbury, who was awarded a Stalin 'peace prize', was recently read over Moscow radio. Among other things, Dr Johnson was quoted as having said in reference to the Boat Race, 'I was ashamed of the fact that an American student was the coxswain of the Oxford crew.' Oxford lost. The English people are saying, 'The presence of an American in the Oxford boat made it sink. The British Navy is now under American command, and under American command Great Britain awaits the same fate that befell the Oxford boat.' Fortunately, however, every time the threatening clouds descend over the world, the voice of Stalin inspires confidence.

11 April 1951

FLEET STREET DUCK'S BROOD DEAD

The mallard duck which succeeded in rearing a family of five at the edge of a static water tank amid the ruins north of Fleet Street sat forlornly on a floating plank yesterday, her five ducklings floating lifeless in the water around her.

The tank, which is at the corner of Pemberton Row and Goldsmiths Street, is about 24 yards long and half as broad and has a high brick wall round it. Beneath the foul-looking water, which is about a foot deep, can be seen slime-covered rubble and old cans. A few rushes have taken root and rustle in the wind. Doors, odd pieces of wood, and decomposing bread float on the surface, together with the scurrying water beetles. There appears to be little vegetable matter on which the ducklings could have fed. As the mother, balanced on one leg, slept in the sunshine yesterday, the fluffy seeds of the rosebay willowherb, blown from the bombed sites, fell around her.

Overlooking the scene is the window of the attic study of Dr Samuel Johnson's house in Gough Square. The little disaster recalls the epitaph to a duckling which was commonly attributed to Johnson when he was only three years old:

> Here lies good master duck,
> Whom Samuel Johnson trod on:
> If it had lived it had been good luck,
> For then we'd had an odd one.

Alas for the duck of Pemberton Row, the noxious substance which is hidden in the static water tank has left her with not even 'an odd one'!

20 August 1951

SEAL IN FAMOUS ROME FOUNTAIN

ROME   Passers-by in the Piazza di Trevi, the square whose main feature is the great fountain into whose waters every visitor who wishes to return to Rome must throw a coin, were astonished this morning to see a seal swimming in the basin. The animal was the property of two Roman journalists, who had brought it back from Sardinia and who apparently thought it suitable that the seal should have a swim in such famous surroundings. A literal-minded policeman fined them for contravening the by-law which prohibits the throwing of anything but money into the fountain, and they and the seal departed in a motor-car.

14 December 1951

'Passers-by were astonished . . .'
[SEAL IN FAMOUS ROME FOUNTAIN]

[*The Messaggero* columnist Gino de Sanctis, nicknamed 'foca' (seal), was the recipient of the seal in question, delivered to him by a fellow journalist. The animal arrived in the *Messaggero* offices in a large crate, together with a huge quantity of ice, which flooded the make-up room and nearly lost an edition of the newspaper.]

TELL-TALE TITLES

VIENNA   The arrest is reported from Bratislava of a girl employed at a nationalized bookshop who by accident or design had arranged some of the books in her department in a manner which the local party watch-dogs considered derogatory to Communist prestige.

The books themselves, to the number of four, were the reverse of defamatory. All of them were standard works written by highly respectable party authors. Indeed, one of them, *Far from Moscow*, was a translation of a Russian Komsomol publication which has also been made into a film.

The trouble was not the books, but the order in which the girl had placed them on the shelf. The first title was *We want to Live*; the second *Far from Moscow*; the third *In the Shadow of the Skyscrapers*, and the fourth *Under a Foreign Flag*.

The story is vouched for by someone who was in Bratislava when the girl was arrested.

14 May 1952

BACK FROM EXTINCTION

The current number of *Oryx*, the magazine published by the Fauna Preservation Society, once again devotes an article to the curious and interesting subject of 'breeding-back' the extinct wild ancestor of a domestic animal. Herr Heinz Heck, in two articles, the first of which was published rather more than a year ago, has now described in general terms, though not in precise detail, the experiments he has carried out at the Hellabrunn Zoological Gardens, Munich, to bring back into

45

existence first the aurochs, a European wild ox the last specimen of which, a cow, died in Poland in 1627, and next the tarpan, a wild horse which became extinct in its last stronghold, the steppes of the Ukraine, no longer ago than 1876. Of neither animal did even a single skin survive in a museum, but of each of them there are paintings, descriptions, and some bones. The aurochs was the ancestor of European domestic cattle. The tarpan has been considered the ancestor of the swift types of riding horse, such as the Arab.

The aurochs bull was black, with a yellowish-white stripe along the back, the cow was red-brown, with a darker neck. They were as big as the largest domestic breed of today, but with longer legs and bigger horns, which were pale, with dark tips. Herr Heck began crossing many sorts of domestic breeds in 1921, and by careful selection had by 1932 produced one bull and one cow of the right type. From these he has bred, without any throw-backs, a stock – now numbering about forty living specimens – which he claims as a re-creation of the aurochs as it was four hundred years ago. Moreover, in Berlin his brother, Professor Lutz Heck, a few years later, using different domestic stocks to breed from, achieved a similar result. As to the tarpan, this was a mouse-grey horse, with slender bones, a short light head, broad forehead, prominent eyes, and – like all truly wild (as opposed to feral) horses – a short, bristly, upstanding mane. Herr Heck chose from Iceland and Gotland mares which were nearest in type to the tarpan; but no domestic horse had the requisite mane, so to obtain it he crossed them with a stallion of Przewalski's horse – the only living wild horse, originally native of Mongolia, but now surviving only in a few zoos. The first foal of the right colour was born in 1933, and as the result of further controlled breeding and selection he claims now to have a stock of 'back-bred' tarpans which – like the aurochs – breed true.

Clearly these experiments are full of controversial possibilities, and their results may perhaps be variously interpreted. Yet at least they are remarkable evidence of the extremely malleable nature of animal form; and, from the point of view of popular eduction, a living re-creation of this kind is a far more vivid and imaginatively stirring demonstration of what an extinct animal looked like than any museum reconstruction could be. Even more remarkable would it be, possibly, if a wild type still existing could be re-created from its domestic descendants. Then the artificially induced reversion could be compared closely, point by point, with the beast in whose breeding man never took a hand, in a way which is impossible with an extinct beast. The wild boar suggests itself for a test of this nature. Work of this sort has been strongly criticized as outside the scope of a zoological garden, but it is not easy to see exactly why. To many people it would seem a valuable experiment if some zoo – say, Whipsnade – would, under full scientific control, attempt to 'breed-back' the wild boar from a selection of domestic pigs.

24 November 1952

GAS CHAMBER TESTS
GYPSIES WERE 'LIKE FLOCK OF SHEEP'

PARIS   The two German physicians, Dr Otto Bickenbach and Dr Eugen Haagen, who were on trial before a military court at Metz for their experiments with human beings from the notorious extermination camp of Struthof, in Alsace, were sentenced tonight to hard labour for life.

Haagen and Bickenbach, the public prosecutor said, did not carry out human experimentation but criminal experiments. Haagen he described as 'a maniac of experimentation, an inquisitor, and a sadist', Bickenbach was 'a so-called scientist', who took part in the selection of 'human guinea-pigs'. He invoked the orders of Himmler, but 'the responsibility of a physician cannot be delegated'.

Bickenbach described yesterday the herding of a group of gypsies into the gas chamber for his 'experiments'.

'Guards led them,' he said. 'I do not think anyone was struck. I heard no screams. They seemed inert beings, like a flock of sheep being led to slaughter. These people were led like prisoners; they neither protested nor screamed. It all took place in a very simple and natural fashion.' He added: 'Naturally they were worried, but I had reassured them.'

47

Bickenbach watched the group through a window. He explained that when he tried on them the third concentration of gas, the most powerful, some began to cough and their eyes streamed, but 'none gave a sign to me to stop'. He claimed that if he had not done what he was told, others would have been cruel. He had 'cut the losses'.

The president asked him why he had volunteered for Strasbourg, where the experiments took place. 'My duty', he replied, 'was to remain at the front, as my place of combat, such as I could assume. And then there was the danger to which my people were subjected, for gas warfare was imminent. That is why I had to carry out this research... My position was really diabolical and tragic.'

Asked why he did not try to sabotage the 'experiments', to save human lives, Bickenbach replied: 'Sabotage? But that would have meant transmitting false information. Suppose it had been used in the event of gas warfare? What a responsibility I would have incurred towards all my compatriots.'

24 November 1952

BRIGHTENING THE TIP OF LONDON

It has been suggested that many of the weather-vanes to be seen in London should be cleaned in time for the Coronation. This modest proposal for brightening the uppermost parts of London escaped even the imaginative authorities of the Festival of Britain, and it is therefore small wonder that few people realize how many weather-vanes are still to be seen in the capital.

Many, of course, are the plain arrows on church steeples, usually with a rather wide vane (or banner) as the tail to catch the wind. There are few weathercocks on London churches, though they are reputed to have been originally an ecclesiastical emblem. Some churches carry the emblem of the saint to whom they are dedicated as a weather-vane, just as St Peter-upon-Cornhill has keys as its design. The tiny City church of

St Ethelburga in Bishopsgate has one of London's few weathercocks, though it is of unusual design, the cock itself forming the whole of one side of the vane, the other side being in the form of a banner bearing the date 1675.

In Bishopsgate also there are weather-vanes of distinctive character on some of the secular buildings. High above St Helen's Place the weather-vane is in the form of a beaver and beyond the gates of the Leathersellers' Company, at the end of the place, a fine antlered head is to be seen. Along Threadneedle Street, where the 'Old Lady' has no weather-vane, is one of the City's most imposing, the giant grasshopper on the Royal Exchange; the insect was the crest of Sir Thomas Gresham. The weather-vane served the same purpose on the predecessor of the present building, and its preservation shows, perhaps, that London has some affection for its weather-vanes.

Ship in Full Sail

That, indeed, is still more clearly shown by the weather-vane of St Michael, Queenhithe, a City church demolished in the last century, being still in use on a building near the site of the church. This attractive vane is in the form of a sailing ship and in former times its hull was reputed to hold a bushel of grain in token of the traffic in corn then carried on at Queenhithe. Another ship in full sail can be seen on a building near London Bridge and, close beside it, is a weather-vane that takes the form of a multi-shafted arrow with a single head.

From London Bridge itself it is pleasant to look downstream towards the Customs House and see the huge fish that make the vanes for Billingsgate Market. They are creatures against which, in point of size, the twin cock pheasants of the Leadenhall Market would have no chance whatever. Beyond Billingsgate the eye alights on the Tower of London with its many banners that turn with the wind, or looking upstream, the unattractive outposts of Cannon Street station on each of which is a plain arrow type of weather-vane that has become a favourite roosting-place for starlings.

A diligent seeker will find many weather-vanes in London comparable with those mentioned and a very old inhabitant would be able to tell him of many more that have disappeared. It would be pleasant to have those that remain cleaned up and given enough oil to make them true.

1 January 1953

[The following March there was much discussion about the newly cleaned weather-vane of 'Lousy St Luke's' in Old Street. The Rev. D. McClean Oldaker, a former incumbent of this church, produced convincing evidence to suggest that, contrary to popular belief, the vane did not depict a louse, but a dragon. Later Mr Oldaker's predecessor Mr Brewer hypothesized that the oddly-shaped vane was neither a louse nor a dragon but a comet, which had appeared while St Luke's was being built, in 1733.]

GERMAN 'FLYING SAUCER'

According to Herr Georg Klein, an engineer who was attached to the Ministry of Munitions during the war, Germany had developed a piloted 'flying saucer', and he himself witnessed the first test flight in Prague in February 1945.

The aircraft, he asserted, attained a height of 40,680 ft within three minutes and a maximum speed of 1,366 miles an hour in level flight. In a statement to *Die Welt am Sonntag* he said that it might seem astonishing that the first flight attained a speed nearly twice as great as that of sound, but with this ideal aerodynamic type it would be possible to reach a speed of 2,485 miles an hour, and even more.

The Prague test, he added, was the result of experiments which began in 1941 and which cost millions of marks. The 'flying saucer', other machines that were being built, and the constructional plans were destroyed just before the Russians marched into Prague. A model designed by Miethe, the constructor of the 'V' weapons, and also the closest of his assistants fell, however, into the hands of the Russians at Breslau. Since the Russians entered Prague there had been no trace of the assistant, Herr Klein said. A test pilot and constructor named Schriever died recently in Bremen, and Miethe, who left Breslau by air at the last moment, is now said to be working in the United States.

1 May 1953

COUPLE'S HOME IN DOG KENNEL

For a year a husband and wife have lived in a wooden dog kennel seven feet long by five feet wide at Ystradmynach, Glamorgan. The kennel is one of four in the corner of a disused allotment. Three are occupied by dogs and the fourth by Mrs Dorothy May Norman and her husband, an engineer at a local power station.

Caerphilly council yesterday gave them a week to leave. Dr W. R. Nash, the medical officer of health, said: 'The position is incompatible with any standard of housing.'

Mr and Mrs Norman moved into the kennel on leaving two rooms in a neighbouring village after failing to obtain another home where they could still breed their prize-winning dogs.

6 June 1953

MARTINIS FOR MARTINEZ

Mr Juan Martinez, a 64-year-old resident of Puerto Rico, is due home at San Juan for breakfast this morning. Mr Martinez, who speaks only Spanish, was to have left New York for Puerto Rico on Sunday afternoon. At the airport, where his boarding ticket showed no flight number, he was mistakenly assisted on board an aircraft bound for Frankfurt, Germany. Asked by the stewardess, who spoke only English, if he would care for a drink, the off-course passenger answered with his name, Martinez, and was promptly served with a dry Martini cocktail.

As the aircraft winged northward instead of southward, this performance was apparently repeated several times before the first port of call, Gander, Newfoundland, was reached. There the error was noticed by Mr Martinez, who, in spite of the abundance of refreshment, detected what appeared to be unusually cool weather for a Caribbean July. After an overnight stay at the airline's expense Mr Martinez returned on a flight from Rome and is now safely on his way to San Juan – apparently still marvelling at the unusually hospitable treatment accorded him on his odyssey.

8 July 1953

DUCKS 'AS NOISY AS MOTOR LORRIES'

In a case which is being heard at the university city of Freiburg-im-Breisgau noise experts have testified that 10 quacking ducks make as much noise as three motor-lorries with trailers. The action has been brought by a boarding house keeper, who complained that the ducks in the municipal park disturbed her guests, and she is asking for redress. Originally the park mustered only seven ducks, but by the end of the summer it boasted of about 40.

This week the city fathers rejected a compromise under which the number would have been reduced to 15 and the smaller colony would have been fed early in the morning to stop their quacking. The local court will sit on 2 October to give judgement. An interim injunction has been granted that until the court gives its decision only 15 of the ducks may roam about the park.

25 September 1953

VICAR'S EXPLANATION OF 'COMMANDMENT'
'NOT AN ATTACK ON TRADE UNIONS'

Dr W. G. Snow, vicar of Bognor Regis, who in a sermon on 19 July gave a 'modern' version of the Ten Commandments, has been informed by the Bishop of Chichester, Dr G. K. A. Bell, of his 'deep regret' that the vicar expressed himself in that way.

The fourth of the 'Commandments' stated: 'Remember that thou goest easy in the evil necessity of work. Five days thou mayest labour with every possible rest for tea. On the sixth day or the seventh thou mayest do overtime, double rates, for this is the law of the union. On the seventh day thou canst please thyself about bed or sport and read the Sunday newspapers.'

Trade unionists in Sussex protested to the Bishop. A letter from Dr Bell was read to a meeting of the Sussex Federation of Trades Councils at Brighton on Saturday. It stated: 'I have seen Dr Snow and told him of my deep regret that he should have expressed himself in the way in which he did so as to endanger the movement for a better understanding between clergy and ministers and representatives of various trade unions in Sussex. He assures me that he had in no way intended his sermon – and particularly the fourth modern commandment in that sermon – as an attack on the trade unions, and he says, "Could I have foreseen the upset to the unions I would certainly have removed all reference to them." '

The Bishop added that in a letter to him Dr Snow had written that he had no intention of slighting honest trade unionists, for whom he had the highest respect.

21 December 1953

ELMS, RAVENS, AND ROOKS

One of the last raven residents of London, apart from the famous Tower colony, lived in Hyde Park during the early years of the nineteenth century, and his quaint biography is linked with one of the elms which is possibly among those scheduled to be felled. His parent birds were the last to nest in the Park, and were descended from the large body of ravens which frequented London until well after the middle of the eighteenth century.

When the young birds were old enough a keeper robbed this nest; the old birds left and did not return, but one nestling, at least, was successfully reared and given the freedom of the Park. Partly tame, it became a great favourite with Londoners, and its favourite haunt was the bridge at the head of the Serpentine. It would allow almost anyone to approach and fondle it; one day a lady crossing the bridge dropped a gold bracelet which the raven seized and flew away with to the top of an elm.

The bracelet was never recovered and so may still lie hidden in some crevice of the elm. The raven was carried off soon after, and it was believed he had been taken by someone who coveted him for a pet. This idea was confirmed when the bird reappeared with one wing clipped. His faith in human beings was apparently destroyed; he had become quite unapproachable and, although he still perched in the old, favourite spot, was moody and morose. One morning he was found drowned in the Serpentine, and those who had sought to resume friendship with him said he had committed bird suicide.

A few ravens continued to visit Hyde Park until about the middle of the nineteenth century; but none nested there again, although ravens remained fairly common in the outskirts of London for some time.

The Temple Rookery

Rooks, however, remained London residents even into the present century. Oliver Goldsmith gave a picturesque account of the unusual origin of one London rookery, that of Temple Gardens. His story has been doubted, but may well be true.

This rookery (Goldsmith says) was established in Queen Anne's reign, when Sir Edward Northey, Attorney-General, decided to bring rooks to the Temple from his Epsom home. His plan was ingenious; he had a bough on which was a nest containing nestlings gently sawn down and lowered to a waiting wagon.

When the branch and nest were carefully secured to the wagon, a little time was allowed for the parent birds to recover from the disturbance and begin to feed the nestlings. The horse wagon then began its slow journey to London, the parent birds circling over it, and they and it arrived at Temple Gardens where the bough was secured to one of the trees chosen as suitable. The nestlings were reared successfully, and, the following year, some rooks' eggs were hatched by a magpie into whose nest the rooks' eggs had been introduced. It would be agreeable to have these statements fully authenticated: and the mere fact (which has been quoted against them) that rooks established themselves in the Temple in 1666 is not necessarily incompatible with what Goldsmith wrote.

There were some dozen other rookeries in inner London. The last to be regularly occupied was that in Gray's Inn, and that was abandoned after 1915.

Whether any of the fellers will come across the bracelet which the raven stole, or if the tree which held it was felled long ago, none can know. Its history, in any event, recalls how Londoners have long loved their bird population, and increasingly so as the great metropolis sprawled ever outwards and made the beautiful parks and animal and bird inhabitants more precious as a link with rural sights and sounds; the echo of Eden in their midst!

19 January 1954

SAVED BY THE CLOCK

Harold Wood, aged 42, a clock engineer, of Leicester, clung to one of the hands on St Mary's Hospital clock, 60 ft above the ground in Oxford Road, Manchester, yesterday when scaffolding fell. He was treated in hospital for slight hand injuries.

While he hung from the clock face for more than 5 minutes his workmates fetched a ladder. Only a short time before, Mr Wood, who was working on a veranda near by, had put screws into the clock hand, which held his weight.

26 February 1954

DUTCHMAN SENTENCED FOR £10,000 FRAUD

Robert Lombert, aged 31, a tailor's son in The Hague, has been sentenced to two and half years' imprisonment for obtaining money by false pretences. He assembled many relatives and other people in a luxurious yacht in which they were to go into exile because of 'the imminent danger of Communism'. He was alleged to have told stories that enabled him to swindle several persons to the tune of more than £10,000.

Lombert said that he was president of a secret international security organization of which Napoleon had been the first president. The organization now had its headquarters in Brussels, with Mr Eugene Black, president of the International Bank, as its treasurer and Sir Winston Churchill as its Secretary of War.

15 June 1954

LEECHES UNRECOGNIZED

A 'nest of young adders' was recently discovered by a farm dog which was digging a hole in its master's garden. Doubts were expressed about the creatures being adders – the farmer thought they might be young slow-worms or blindworms – but to be on the safe side, and for the sake of the dog and the children, the squirming mass was brought, in a jam jar, for my opinion.

They were not young adders, nor even slow-worms, but leeches, which the countryman regards as pond-life and would not recognize on terra firma. In this district of Surrey, however, we have not only the ordinary leech, which lives most of its life in ponds, but the European land-leech, which when fully grown is much larger and a fine dark green in colour.

It is said to prey on earthworms, and at one time to have pursued them over the flower beds and along the gravel walks of Regent's Park. A fine specimen brought to me by a neighbour some years ago was found rampaging down a garden path, and my gardener who saw it said that he had sometimes dug up such creatures.

1 July 1954

[How many readers, I wonder, have been pursued down the gravel paths of Regent's Park by marauding leeches? I shall never go near the place again.]

AMERICAN'S FLIGHT UNDER LONDON BRIDGE

LE HAVRE   Mr Gene Thompson, the American who flew a small aero club aircraft between the towers of Tower Bridge and under London Bridge yesterday, was today on board the Panamanian passenger ship Atlantic bound for New York. Mr Thompson, a former United States Air Force pilot who served in Korea, told a reporter on board the ship that he had taken the mono-plane up to impress his friend Miss Helen Brown, a 22-year-old student from Texas. He explained that immediately after landing the aircraft he took the train for Southampton and boarded the ship 'with all possible speed'.

13 August 1954

ATOMIC AUTHORITY'S COAT OF ARMS

The Atomic Energy Authority has adopted a coat of arms symbolizing the peaceful uses of atomic power. Savage heraldic animals chained to the earth represent the power of the atom brought under control. Stars on each animal have a total of 92 points, symbolizing uranium – No 92 in the list of chemical elements. An inverted triangle on the shield is a heraldic symbol called a 'pile', the first name for an atomic reactor or power furnace. Zigzag lines represent electricity developed from atomic energy.

On top of the helmet, which is a symbol of cooperation, a sun signifies the benign power of the atom. The bird inside the sun is a sign taken from the crest of the late Lord Rutherford, one of the world's most distinguished pioneers in nuclear research. The motto chosen by the Atomic Energy Authority is *Maxima E Minimis*, meaning 'the most from the smallest.'

18 February 1955

ARISTOPHANES EDITION IMPOUNDED IN US

A copy of a limited English edition of Aristophanes's *Lysistrata* has been impounded by the United States Post Office as unfit to pass through the mail. 'Plainly lewd, obscene and lascivious' is the Postmaster-General's description of the book. The edition was first published in England in 1927 by the Fanfrolico Press and consists of a verse translation by Mr Jack Lindsay with illustrations by his father, the Australian artist Mr Norman Lindsay. Four or five copies of it are believed already to be in American libraries.

The bookseller to whom the book was consigned last August has lodged a court appeal for its release and for a declaration that the power of the Post Office to censor 'art and literature' is unconstitutional. His lawyer has asked the court, in a vigorously worded brief, 'by what right does our prurient Post Office think to censor the magnificent Aristophanes, poet, political reformer, social uplifter, philosophical thinker with a dozen titles to immortality? By what authority does our Postmaster translate sex into sin... *Lysistrata* into pornography?'

The Post Office has declined to comment on the matter.

7 March 1955

GERMAN CARICATURE OF 'THE TIMES'

A cartoon in *Die Welt* expresses indignation at a suggestion recently put forward by *The Times*. The cartoon shows an elderly lady, forbiddingly drawn with a spiky, bespectacled nose almost meeting her sharp chin, with one thin arm raised in admonition and the other hand drawing a small boy, clearly in her charge, away from the temptation of playing with an urchin. The urchin is labelled 'east zone' and the other boy 'Federal Republic', and he is saying : 'Why mustn't I, Auntie?' The good woman's clothes are made of newsprint, and on the top of her bonnet the words 'The Times' are legible.

The reference is to a leading article in *The Times* of 22 April which included the suggestion that if no agreement on German unity was in sight it was just possible that a four-Power conference might agree to limit the arms in each part of Germany. *Die Welt* takes this to be an admission that German hopes for reunification have been written off as too difficult to realize, and in their place a proposal put forward which 'can never find acceptance in Germany'.

28 April 1955

BLOWING HIS OWN TRUMPET

A West Riding schoolmaster's unusual request – for the supply of an Alp horn – has sent a loud blast through the corridors of the County Hall, Wakefield and caused some interesting departmental correspondence.

Officials at County Hall declined to divulge the name of the school for which the horn was requested, but the education committee's schools bulletin states that the school gives housecraft and woodwork lessons to pupils from surrounding schools. Sometimes a teacher is unexpectedly absent and the children make a fruitless journey. By using an Alp horn the headmaster would be able to send an unmistakable signal to the surrounding hills and prevent unnecessary travel.

The note of the divisional educational officer was: 'I gather that Alp horns vary in length from 10 ft to 18 ft and, naturally,

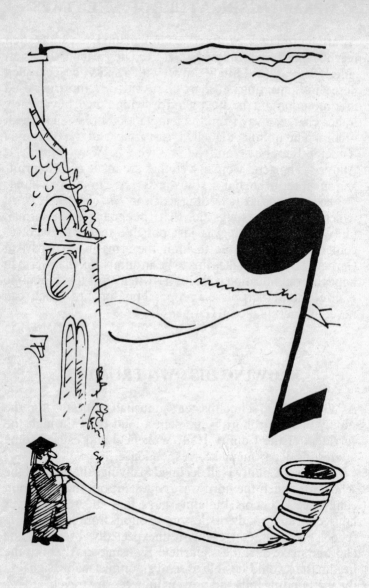

'An unmistakable signal . . .'
[BLOWING HIS OWN TRUMPET]

the longer the horn the better the fundamental note. We should like a deep note, but not too deep, and I can confirm that it is the Swiss kind we wish to have and not the sort used in the Himalayas or South America. Incidentally, the headmaster is rather attracted by the velvet jacket shown in your photograph, and although these are obviously not essentials, we do think we ought to do the thing properly if at all.'

Supply of Uniform

In his reply the head of the county supplies department, Mr N. Calvert, says: 'I cannot at this stage give a firm quotation for the supply of an Alp horn, nor for the supply of a uniform for the use of the horn blower. An instrument of the authentic Swiss type would perhaps have to be imported from Switzerland, and the cost is, I understand, likely to be in the region of £30. I have no reason to suppose that the Himalayan or South American type would be less expensive.

'If you wish alternative signalling devices such as a set of tom tom drums (which might simplify the problem of appropriate clothing for the operator, since a tin of black greasepaint might suffice) or some visual mechanical, electrical or radio signalling apparatus to be considered, no doubt you will let me know. I assume that you would also obtain the necessary consent from the police authorities for the use of any audible signalling device.'

The final comment comes from the education department: 'As this item costs more than £10 and might involve the committee in heavy maintenance costs, to wit, travelling expenses from Interlaken for a horn tuner, the divisional education officer might be asked for a confirmation of the approval of the school governors before the request is submitted to the committee.'

24 May 1955

[On the following 28 June an Alp horn arrived as a gift from a *Times* reader in Switzerland.]

BULLET THROUGH BRAIN CAUSED A HEADACHE

PRETORIA   'A million-to-one chance' is how doctors describe the escape this weekend of a young African who was shot through the back of his head by a revolver bullet which emerged above his eyes without doing more than give him a headache. Doctors say the bullet passed between the lobes of the brain as it 'breathed'. After being shot, the native walked some distance and an hour or two later made a statement to police in hospital. He also identified his assailant. Today he was progressing well.

9 August 1955

LIGHTING THE STREET LAMPS OF LONDON

The sight of the lamplighter with the long pole turning the dark streets at dusk into a pattern of yellow lights, now becoming rarer, had a childhood fascination for me, and it still persists. From a chance meeting with a friendly artist I learnt that beside a nucleus of 'old timers' there had grown up an outer fringe of lamplighters – painters and writers who found the irregular hours suited their other interests. My friend persuaded me to go to the North Thames Gas Board, and there I was enrolled.

I was told to report to the afternoon muster. This was a rendezvous at the back of a church behind the Albert Hall. I found the appropriate steps and descended into what might have been a crypt. In a murky atmosphere, in the shadow of a forbidding furnace, I shook hands with the muster, three beside myself, and the foreman. They were regulars and I was the novice. I put down my shiny new satchel feeling like the first day at school.

A Strange Torch

'This will be your torch,' said the foreman. I glanced at the 7-ft metal pole. 'You'd better learn to prepare it.'

Not everybody realizes that some of London's lamps are still lit by gas; I had only to watch the faces of people at a bus stop when there was a lamp to be lit directly overhead. The eyes of the queue would follow my torch as I raised it. When the lamp broke into light an answering smile of appreciation and surprise would break out on the upturned faces.

The 'torch' used for this had a trigger at one end and a petrol and oil mechanism at the other. When the trigger was depressed a small flame from the wick at the top was elongated like a tongue to ignite the mantles. In the old days, I believe, they used to put a sulphur match on the top of the torch.

I had about 160 lamps to light and put out. To the uninitiated, street lamps appear to lie in straight lines, but to the lamplighter they turn out to be in a zigzag pattern in which he crosses and recrosses from corner to kerb, from kerb to house, from house to mews, from mews to square and back again, embracing his district with a prescribed minimum of walking.

The Nightly Round

Come with me then on my evening patrol. From east of the Albert Hall we go down Kensington Road, lighting one side as far as the taxi rank, then cross the road and light a small cul-de-sac, back again, not forgetting the traffic islands, and on down towards the Scotch House. Two more alleys, and then, in Knightsbridge proper, a very tall lamp for which I produce the extension pole. This fits into the base of the torch making it about 10 ft long, with a piece of string extending in a Heath Robinson arrangement from the trigger. If it was a windy night and perhaps raining as well, there was always a chance of the small wick flame being blown out as one walked from lamp to lamp. Against this misfortune we were provided with three free boxes of matches a week.

Sometimes, like the Pied Piper, I had a number of children following me, and to mothers who simpered too enthusiastically in urging their children to watch, I would turn and say, 'Would you like *your* child to grow up to be a lamplighter?'

In Knightsbridge there was always a fresh shop-window to look at, a new dress or display. In Montpelier and Trevor Squares there were the interior scenes like a Dutch painting, clearly lit before the curtains were drawn. 'Why was the old lady so late with her tea today?' or 'The Christmas cards are looking nice, but where will they put the rest?'

Down in Kinnerton Mews I fumbled in the dark with each of the two lamps which represented the last outposts of my beat. In Lowndes Square I had to inspect and count the lights which, though gas, were lit by automatic time devices. Smoking a cigarette I would stand beneath the last lamp waiting for it much as one waits for the last train home – thinking of my return to the crypt.

Once back there, each of us filled in his duty book for the day. This included an extinguishing and lighting report, which ended with the poetic sentence, 'Patrolled all refs. and bollards and L/C.'

The extinguishing patrol worked in a very different atmosphere. There was little traffic and no audience. I charged along the pavement on my bicycle, this time with a wooden pole. In the manner of a cavalry tent-peg tilter I knocked each lamp's gascock with the tip of my lance as I drew alongside it. Only the inconsiderate motorist who parked for the night directly under a lamp could spoil the technique. The jagged skyline of roofs slowly came into focus. Occasionally I exchanged a chirrupy greeting with a paper boy: toward the end of the round the early risers were creeping out.

Each week I was responsible for cleaning 103 lamps. This was certainly the backbone of the job; it involved getting used to an extension ladder and riding with it on a bicycle, a feat I never quite mastered; also manipulating with care the large glass globes of those lamps named 'Rochesters', as they were detached for cleaning. One of my special curses was the pair of lamps outside the Royal Thames Yacht Club. So far from being shipshape the glass panels of these lacked putty and were liable to fold up suddenly like a collapsing sail. By Daimler Hire I had to prop my ladder in the middle of the road: lorries were fairly considerate but taxis in malicious mood barely skirted it.

Unsympathetic Friends

Once or twice on patrol I met my friends – the first couple were not romantic in their response: 'How are you?' 'Very well,

thank you.' 'What's that you're carrying?' 'That's my torch.'
'I say – you light lamps. What a game! Sooner you than me!' I
thought with envy of Charlie Chaplin's delightful answer to
the unfriendly thief when Chaplin was a policeman: how he
jumped on a street lamp and with unholy strength bent it down
imprisoning his persecutor's head and turning on the gas – but
my victims were already walking away. The next couple were
rather more sympathetic and waited to see my spectacular bid
with the extension pole outside the Scotch House.

As I bicycled home one night after the evening patrol the
new moon had risen in the velvet sky. Her pale crescent
seemed to stare at me balefully. 'Who are you,' she asked, 'to
steal my light, and cast your yellow glimmer over the city?'
'Never mind,' I answered, 'you can enjoy the last laugh when I
rise grumpily from my bed in tomorrow's dawn to put the darn
things out!'

11 October 1955

'VANISHING INK' CHARGE DISMISSED

PARIS   An examining magistrate today dismissed a complaint that Mr Aristotle Onassis, the Greek shipowner, used
vanishing ink to sign a contract. The complaint was made in
November 1954 by Mr Spyridon Catapodis concerning com-
missions in connexion with Mr Onassis's contract to carry
Saudi Arabian oil in his tankers.

21 March 1956

[This terse summary hardly does justice to the amazing
vanishing ink affair. Catapodis's *complaint* was dismissed, but the vanishing ink was indeed used, in the
extraordinary affair of the Saudi-Arabian tanker deal. A
full account will be found in Frischauer, Willi, *Onassis*
(Bodley Head, 1968).]

THE ABOMINABLE SNOWMAN UNMASKED

The problem of the 'Abominable Snowman', which has

troubled western explorers of the Himalayas since the first Mount Everest expedition of 1921, seems at last to have been cleared up – and in a way satisfactory to honour and sanity.

That it was in need of clearing up has been shown lately by Dr W. L. Strauss, of The Johns Hopkins University, Baltimore: 'During recent years stories have been coming out of India and Tibet about a giant mammal that lives above the snow line. According to some accounts, this creature is more than 7 ft in height, walks erect, has an apelike head and face, and is covered with heavy blonde or reddish hair . . . the implication is that it is some sort of giant primate. Huge footprints in the snow, at heights of from 10,000 ft to 21,000 ft above sea level, and attributed to the "snowman", have been reported by a variety of people . . . From Himalayan expeditions have come actual photographs of the footprints.'

Langur Monkey Puzzle

The British Museum (Natural History) has entered twice into the argument. In 1937 tracks photographed by Dr F S Smythe in the Garhwal Himalayas were identified by the late Mr R. I. Pocock as those of the 'Red Bear', *Ursus arctos isabellinus*. In 1951 tracks photographed by Mr Eric Shipton were said to be not those of a bear but more probably of the langur monkey, *Presbytis entellus achilles*, and an exhibition in support of this theory was arranged at the museum. Later, two Norwegian engineers, Aage Thorberg and Jan Frostis, while prospecting for uranium for the Indian Government, had an encounter with two langur-like animals, one of which bit Frostis.

The most recent contributor is Sreemat Swami Pranavananda, an Indian religious notable, who has travelled much in the Himalayas and Tibet, has received support in his geographical work from the survey of India, and in an account published in the *Indian Geographical Journal* gives the impression of being careful and critical in his collection of information. His account seems almost conclusive on the main point: that, whatever other animals may leave tracks above the snow line, the animal of the legend is the red bear.

Man-Bear Mistranslated

Sreemat Pranavananda states that the red bear, familiar to Tibetan shepherds as an animal, is known to them usually as the *mi-te* ('man-bear', because it walks on its hind legs), but sometimes as the *kangmi* ('snowman'). These two, alternative, names being combined, the first – which can also be written as *mi-tre*, with a very lightly sounded *r* – had been mistranslated (as if without this fine distinction of sound) as 'abominable, filthy, or disgusting'. So the 'Abominable Snowman' was born. The Sreemat emphasizes also that Tibetan shepherds distinguish the *mi-te*, as an animal and in speech, from two other bears; and that the main cause of confusion was lack of thorough investigation on the Tibetan side of the Himalayas.

He first heard of the *mi-te* in 1935 from a Tibetan shepherd pilgrim who told him of attacks on sheep in a place, the Kyang Chhu, which is at 16,000 ft altitude; when fired at, it had at first run off on all fours, and later stood up on its hind legs. It was as tall as a man, and light or reddish brown in colour. Two years later he received a similar report from one of the headstreams of the Brahmaputra. However, the most detailed account had come to him in July 1953, in response to a request to Tibetan friends in the Manas region to collect information by offer of a reward. The most circumstantial in its tying-up of name, animal, and footprints was of a *mi-te* which in February of that year visited a camp at 15,000 ft, on the Tag Tsangpo, on the south-east side of Manasarovar. It was seen in the valley, moving sometimes on all fours, and sometimes on its hind legs. The account was as follows:

'The footprints of the *mi-te* left on the hard ground scantily covered by sand measured 16 fingers or 11 in. in length, and 7 fingers or 5 in. in breadth. The legs (i.e. hind legs) had five toes each, and the hands (*lhakpa*) only four toes, or only four toes could be seen in the imprints . . . The toes were two fingers or 1½ in. long . . . The animal when on its hind legs was described as being taller than a tall man. The colour of the bear was dark brown, though the shade varies from one part of the body to another. The body of the animal is covered with a thick coat of reddish brown hair and the hairs on the face are pretty long. Ten days after, when the shepherds had gone up the valley, they marked the footprints of the *mi-te* on the snow fields to be a subit (18 in.) in length and corresponding width, with no traces of toes.'

Said to Attack Yak

Mi-te were also reported to attack yak, and man when alone, and often to make excursions into the snow fields and on to glaciers. He himself had found vegetation at heights up to about 20,000 ft; and in regard to the enlargement of track marks by the melting of snow round the edges, he had been able to connect 21-in. footprints in a difficult and rarely used pass with the passage of a lama through it some 25 days earlier. He had also an unconfirmed report of hibernation by the *mi-te* under rocks or in a cave.

On this evidence, supporting his own directly obtained reports, he concludes that the 'so-called "Abominable Snowman"' is none other than the red bear of the Himalayas. But it is not alone in leaving tracks on the high snow. Tracks of other animals such as those of the wild yak, the Tibetan wild horse, Tibetan antelope, and musk deer, he saw, sometimes for miles on end, during the winters of 1935–7 and 1943–4. Other possibilities were the lynx, snow leopard, and wolf. But he is sceptical about the langur, which 'mostly get down to warmer regions much before the snowfall'. That may be their usual behaviour. But 'snowman' or no, there remain the British Museum identification and the later Norwegian encounter; at biting range, even two university-trained engineers seem unlikely to have taken any other animal for a monkey.

3 July 1956

ACTION BY EAU DE COLOGNE MAKERS

The manufacturers of 4711 eau de Cologne are bringing an action against a Herr Koelsch, of Siegen, on the ground that he is damaging the interests of their business. Herr Koelsch makes a living from emptying cesspits and happens to have the telephone number 4711, which he exhibits prominently on his van. He claims that he was given the number purely by chance, and is insisting on his right to have it painted in large letters on his vehicle. The case is coming up before a Cologne court on Wednesday.

9 July 1956

DOCTOR'S DOG WATCH

Time passes slowly in our valley. As a country doctor I have seen many comings and goings. But it was a genuine pleasure for all of us to welcome the young Canadian couple when they came to live in Rose Cottage on the edge of our village green. He was something to do with ecology at the local scientific research station down by the lake, while she wafted all the fresh air and charm of the Maritime Provinces into our English lives. But tadpoles and water snails make dull pets around the house, so our new friends swung to the other extreme and bought a bloodhound puppy. For the best part of a year the trio vied with each other in mutual adoration.

Alas, even the most equilateral triangle can never be eternal; our ecologist was flown back to Canada in the fall for a university lecture tour, leaving his conjugal and canine relics in mournful possession of Rose Cottage. He also left his wrist-watch on the dressing table. His grass widow dutifully ate out her soul with remorse, but the bloodhound went one better. It proved its devotion by eating the wrist-watch, and that was how the National Health Service came into the picture. We usually X-ray the tummies of kids who swallow drawing-pins, and it seemed only fair to do the same for the bloodhound.

Wary Approach

In the good old days of private practice a box of chocolates would have squared the staff nurse in the X-ray department of our cottage hospital to take pictures of anything, but now with management committees and all that sort of administrative nonsense we have to tread more warily in spending public funds. That was why patient, owner, and doctor slid through the tradesmen's entrance at 8 o'clock last Sunday morning, and we should have completed a full set of films in half an hour if the patient had not scented matron's cat on the stairs.

Viewed academically as a hunt it was a first-class show. Up the length of the women's surgical ward, on through the operating theatre, down to the kitchen, with the night porter hulloaing a check by the lift shaft. Puss went to earth in the mortuary. Rather than risk further scandal by putting in the gardener's terrier, we made a discreet retirement and hoped that the patients would cover up, as they usually did, for the eccentricities of the visiting medical staff. Although Matron never heard as much as a whisper about the whole affair, we thought it might be wiser to abandon the conventional idea of X-ray control of the progress of the patient's foreign body.

That left us in a bit of a quandary. The wrist-watch was luminous. The recent Government publications on the hazards of nuclear radiation had been rather frightening about microcuries bombarding certain delicate parts of the body, and there we were landed with the cherished puppy speeding itself on towards sterility. We borrowed a geiger counter from the research laboratory, but the wretched thing clicked inconclusively all over the bloodhound's abdomen.

I brushed aside such newfangled techniques and fell back upon that trusted symbol of the physician's art, the stethoscope. Auscultation localized the watch in the greater curvature of the stomach. At least that was the area portrayed in the lurid diagram of a dog's anatomy in a tattered Canadian dictionary. While someone leaned on the patient's head we marked the spot with a ball point pen.

Inactive Treatment

Masterly inactivity seemed the obvious line of treatment for the rest of the day, until it suddenly occurred to me that once the mainspring unwound we should again lose our control of progress. Careful inquiry resolved that worry. The watch had one of those self-winding devices to rejuvenate itself with the movement of the wearer's wrist. We organized the neighbours into shifts to trot the bloodhound round the village green every two hours, with an extra lap up to the post office at dusk. We bedded the patient down on the rocking chair and prayed for a restless night. At breakfast time my stethoscope listened anxiously. The tick was there, but still depressingly beneath the ink splash on the hound's abdominal wall. We went on winding and waiting.

By the evening of the third day I felt just about ready to call in consultant veterinary opinion when the ticking suddenly shifted to the zone where my human patients usually get their appendicitis. By morning it was well over the mid line, and by noon we had the watch back, still ticking faithfully. It seems a pity that delicacy prevents the watchmakers from taking full advantage of the advertisement value of their hardy product. Whenever I gaze into a city jeweller's shop window and see a wrist-watch suspended in a tank of water I raise my hat in silent tribute.

7 September 1956

AN EAR TO THE RAIL

In future, west German drivers may be liable to dismount at open level crossings and put an ear to the rail to ensure that a train is not approaching before crossing, if the ruling of a local court at Nordhorn, North Rhine-Westphalia, becomes a precedent.

This ruling was made by the Nordhorn magistrates' court recently when a lorry driver appeared after an accident at a crossing. It was misty at the time and the driver stopped, but seeing no train drove over the crossing. Unfortunately, a train emerged from the mist and collided with the lorry's trailer.

The driver was found Guilty of negligence for not listening for an approaching train in Red Indian fashion. The Allgemeine Deutsche Automobil-Club, alarmed by the prospects of roads clogged with vehicles while drivers kneel at the rails, has offered to pay the man's legal costs.

26 March 1957

FARMER INHALED PART OF WHISTLE

A farmer, aged 35, who inhaled part of a whistle while dancing at a Christmas Eve party carried the plastic mouthpiece in his bronchus for 10 months. 'He developed a wheeze,' states the *Lancet*, reporting the case this week.

After the party, the farmer found that forceful exhalation produced a slight whistling sound from the right side of the chest. On arrival at hospital about two hours after the accident, radiography revealed a metallic reed in the lower lobe of his right lung. The reed was easily removed. The patient's statement that he had inhaled a plastic whistle was discounted, partly because of his somewhat convivial state on admission.

About two months later the farmer developed a wheeze and later a cough and slight chest pain. Nine months after the party gangrene was found in the bronchus. He was transferred to a chest hospital and the mouthpiece of the whistle was then found and removed with some difficulty.

12 April 1957

WIDTH OF ATLANTIC A MILITARY SECRET

WASHINGTON   After spending four years recharting the North Atlantic the United States Air Force has pinpointed Europe's position in relation to that of the North American continent, but is withholding the information for security reasons. A spokesman said that the Air Force would like to disclose whether the two continents were farther apart or nearer than was supposed, but such information would be of great military value to Russia.

9 May 1957

SLEEP AT THE TURN OF A SWITCH

A Moscow factory is now producing a machine which is said to be capable of inducing sleep electrically. The machine was devised at the Soviet Institute of Experimental Surgical Apparatus.

It is being used in cases of insomnia, high blood pressure, ulcers, and other ailments.

Its designer, Mr Yuri Hudi, said in a recent interview that a rubber helmet is placed over the patient's head, with electrodes which are applied to the back of the head and to the eye sockets. Sleep is induced by rhythmic impulses of a weak electric current passing through the cerebral cortex, causing inhibition in the cells.

Inhibition means sleep, Mr Hudi said, and the deeper the slumber the less the resistance of the tissues to the current. A glance at meters on the control mechanism reveals how fast asleep a patient is.

17 May 1957

[Three days later *The Times* revealed that a certain Professor S. Braines who had been working at the laboratories of the Soviet Academy of Medical Science had prolonged the life of a 15-year-old senile dog to 21 years by three months' artificial sleep. It was stated that the animal's sex instinct had been gradually restored in the process.]

MY FIRST CUTTLEFISH

The designers of bedrooms with windows facing east should, I had always thought, be certified as anti-social. This morning, however, as the sun peeped over the hedge at the bottom of the garden and shone in my face, instead of pulling the clothes over my head, turning over and going to sleep again, I found myself accepting the invitation. It was the matter of a moment to slip into some slacks and half-wellingtons and there I was, slightly astonished at myself, pedalling to the beach.

When I reached the beach, I had never seen the tide so far out. The sands pink, brown and virginal, stretched out invitingly seawards. Some rooks, oyster-catchers, and black-backed gulls, engaged in picking over some shells, took to the air noisily and I was alone on the sand.

First I walked along the high tide mark and was made immediately aware of an offensive, fishy smell. Every yard or so there was a flat, putrefying piece of flesh, in appearance not unlike the upper of a very ancient gym shoe. Each adhered to or enclosed the familiar cuttlebone. The sand fleas were busily engaged in cleaning up what the crabs had left, and soon all that would be left as proof of this mass destruction would be cuttlebones by the thousand. These no doubt would be collected to make toothpowder or fertiliser or for feeding to canaries.

A Rare Sight

I turned towards the sea and wondered whether the recent strong and persistent north-easterly wind was to blame for this unusual invasion and high casualty rate. Cuttlefish are occasionally seen in the flesh on English shores but to see thousands of them is rare indeed. Apart from a strong supposition that they emigrate to the shallow waters in the spring and early summer to breed, their movements and habits are largely unknown, though the Mediterranean fisherfolk seem better informed. They maintain one certain way of attracting the male cuttlefish is to tow a female on a line from the stern of a boat.

As the tide turned I reached the mouth of the estuary. Some foam bubbles swirled slowly past me, twirled in a gentle circle, and then crept back slowly upstream. There was life everywhere in the still, lucid water. Crabs of every size and colour were busy under every piece of oarweed. And then I saw him.

He was almost motionless, some 6 ft from the water's edge. The hump of his head occasionally broke the completely flat surface and sent a slow ripple over the water. Very slowly, he came towards me and I saw at close quarters and for the first time a fine healthy cuttlefish in the prime of life. We eyed each other at a range of about 4 ft but he was unafraid. He flexed his tentacles, wrapped them into a neat, streamlined bunch rather after the manner of a shopwalker washing his hands, took a side-long glance at me and then gently, in an absurdly gracious way, undulated backwards upstream.

The thick flat body, marbled in brown and some 14 in. long, was bordered all round by a narrow willowy fin. It was the undulation of this fin that propelled my cuttlefish. The head, the size of a cricket ball, was sunk, neckless, on the body and from round the mouth protruded the tentacles – five pairs in all. A shimmer of light green flashed from the white underside as the side fins lifted. There was no mistaking him.

He was *Sepia officinalis* – the commonest cuttlefish in these waters, the mighty hunter of prawns. He would use his long pair of tentacles to seize the unwary prawn, shooting them out to their full extended length of nearly a foot. The prawn would then be transferred to the shorter arms and held by the powerful suckers while the hard mouth tore the victim to bits. Not a nice creature, but survival in the sea is no kidglove business.

Cloud of Ink

With my stick I made him alter course towards me. This annoyed him. He dived to the bottom and turned again upstream. Again he was turned and a couple of smart taps on the centre of his back produced the expected reaction – a cloud

75

of black ink. For a matter of seconds he was quite invisible. Then his brown body emerged and the performance was repeated four times, the last being but a feeble cloud of ink. His first line of defence was exhausted.

I flicked him out of the water and had to step quickly aside – a jet of water under considerable pressure was squirted past my head from the mantle cavity on his under-belly. This evolution he was able to do twice without refilling. I refloated him and, as if he understood what I was wanting, he went through his entire swimming repertoire. He undulated – first backwards, then forwards. He dived, he climbed, he rolled. He hung motionless. He suddenly whizzed forward jet-propelled, using his powerful squirt. I only just managed to retrieve him. And then he looked at me and his whole attitude seemed to say – 'Haven't you finished yet? I'm tired.'

I flipped him out on to the pebbles again, avoided the squirt, and examined his tentacles and the suckers on them – how beautiful Nature is down to the minutest detail! Curiosity satisfied, I returned him to the sea. Slowly and with dignity, he swam away. Was it my imagination or was his last backward glance just a little baleful?

17 June 1957

RESTING ON ONE LEG

DARWIN   In what must be one of the most unusual scientific studies ever undertaken, an attempt is being made here to discover why Australian aborigines often stand on one leg to rest – like birds of the stork family. A Sydney orthopaedic specialist, Dr S. H. Scougall, is leading a research party into Arnhem Land to investigate the phenomenon.

Dr Scougall said today that the only theory so far advanced was that the one-legged stance had been an alert, defensive position of rest during the primitive life of the aborigines and had survived. After the natives have been interviewed, a number of white men will be trained to stand on one leg so that an electromiography study can be made.

18 July 1957

'. . . like birds of the stork family'
[RESTING ON ONE LEG]

SOCKS INSIDE OUT 'SCARE WITCHES'

Such apparently illogical happenings as a car steering-wheel smeared with marmalade, a footballer with his stockings turned inside out, or a girl who dropped her glove and failed to thank the person who handed it back to her were explained in a paper dealing with folk-lore to the archaeology and anthropology section.

The speaker was Mr Peter Opie, joint editor of the *Oxford Dictionary of Nursery Rhymes*, who for the past seven years has been conducting a survey into the folk-lore current among English schoolchildren.

The young footballer, he explained, was taking part in a rite nearly 300 years old: in 1659 James Howell wrote: 'Wear the inside of thy stockings outside to scare the witches.' The marmalade on the steering-wheel was part of the 'mischief night' celebrations traditional in Yorkshire, and the apparently ill-mannered girl was perpetuating an old belief that to say 'Thank you' when a glove is retrieved brings bad luck.

Mr Opie contrasted the state of folk-lore scholarship in England with what had been done in Scotland and Ireland. England, he said, was the only one of those countries so uninterested in herself that she had not yet commissioned one full-time folklorist. There was a vast archive of material which, he proposed, should be compiled on historical principles into a dictionary of English folk-lore.

Another speaker, Mr Sean O'Sullivan, described the work of the Irish Folk-lore Commission, by whom he is employed as an archivist. The commission has been in existence since 1935 and sends its own recording van around the country to collect examples of speech, tales, and song. A card index had been compiled and already had 300,000 references.

11 September 1957

CAMEL 'TAUGHT TO SMOKE'

LAHORE A West Pakistan man has appealed to the High Court to call a camel as a witness as the only way of proving his innocence. He had taught his camel to smoke, he said. Asking the court to offer the camel a hookah, he said that if it did not puff at the pipe, he would willingly serve a lower court sentence of five years' imprisonment for stealing the beast. The court is considering his appeal.

25 October 1957

TYPED NOTES FROM 'GOD'

TEL AVIV   Rabbi Ovadia Barati, who produced messages alleged to have come from God and the Archangels promising King Solomon's crown to a credulous business man, was sent to prison today for 18 months for obtaining money by false pretences. Both the rabbi and his victim, Mr Meoded Barzilai, are Yemenite Jews.

The court heard an incredible story of magical rites at midnight, 'fire tests', and sacrifices in the village of Akir not far from the Weizmann Institute, Israel's most up-to-date centre of science and learning.

Test of Faith

Mr Barzilai, who is a partner in an estate agents' firm and owner of a chain of cinemas, said he was promised by the rabbi that the Archangels Gabriel, Raphael, and Michael would anoint him Messiah and King of Israel. He parted altogether with £I 10,000 (£2,000): when he asked what the angels wanted money for, he was told it was merely 'a test of his faith'. He was given three parcels of gold and two suitcases with the throne and robes of Solomon – all of which were not to be opened until 'a sign is given'.

After a series of these transactions he dared the wrath of the angels and opened the packages – only to find pieces of rock and roof tiles. The rabbi told him the treasures had been changed into these worthless objects to punish him for disobedience.

Token Repayment

Finally he sent an 'ultimatum to the Almighty' – either he must immediately be made Messiah, or all his money must be returned. The typewritten reply told him to return any letters he had kept and offered a token repayment of £1 100.

Experts said the 32 letters 'signed' by 'God Almighty' were written on the rabbi's typewriter. They were typed in red. The return address was 'care of Rabbi Barati'.

19 November 1957

BREAKNECK TEMPO

HELSINKI   A young Finnish conductor, Mr Paavo Berglund, broke his neck last Monday at an orchestra rehearsal. Mr Berglund has a habit of shaking his head a little when conducting *forte* passages. A piano concerto by the Finnish composer, Usko Merilainen, which was being played, has a number of *forte* passages and when the conductor was looking sideways to the soloist during one of these he shook his head and felt a sharp pain. Doctors after an X-ray examination put his neck in plaster.

7 February 1958

HERE LIMPS THE BRIDE

A wedding on Saturday at Rochester, New York, is to have some unusual features. The bride, Miss Suzanne Archibald, will be wearing a splint on her foot because of a toe broken in a motoring accident; the bridegroom, Mr Edward Stanton, knocked unconscious in the same accident, is still suffering from concussion, and the maid of honour, who was also in the accident, has a black eye and a sprained ankle. Two of the bridesmaids, victims of skating accidents, have each an arm in a sling, one because of a fractured humerus, the other because of a dislocated shoulder.

14 February 1958

COUPLE LIVED IN TREE TRUNK

Mrs Doris Mary Parkes, aged 37, who has been living in a tree

'They appeared very happy . . .'
[COUPLE LIVED IN TREE TRUNK]

trunk, and was remanded for a week at Worcester today on a charge of stealing a pair of men's boots, told the Magistrates: 'I want to go home.' Bail was refused because the woman could not produce a suitable surety.

The hollow tree in which the woman has lived with her husband is some 25 ft to 30 ft high, about six to seven feet in diameter at the foot, tapering to the top. A split provides an entrance.

Mr T. R. Bomford, farmer and market gardener, of Allesboro farm, Pershore, on whose land the tree stands about 50 yards from the farm house, said in evidence the couple were formerly employed doing casual work on the farm. They were occupying a caravan before living in the tree.

'I was amazed when they first started to live in the tree,' he said. 'I have tried to get them off the land for some time. I have tried every measure to get them out and have even endeavoured to fire the tree in their absence. I have seen the couple there and they appeared very happy.'

19 March 1958

TRIPE FOR THE QUEEN

A restaurant owner at Caen, a founder of the Normandy gastronomic society which glories in the title of 'La Triperie d'Or', has received a letter of thanks and acknowledgement from the British Embassy in Paris on behalf of the Duke of Edinburgh, to whom the proud artist in tripe had sent by post a tureen of tripes *à la mode de Caen*. He enclosed a message apologizing to the Duke for having chosen him as 'ambassador to the Queen for the Triperie d'Or'.

The letter of thanks says the dispatch of the tripe 'gave much pleasure to Prince Philip and to her Majesty the Queen, who were very touched by the friendliness of your gesture'. There is no indication whether this justly famous regional dish was actually consumed by the Queen and the Duke, but the British Embassy's letter concludes by conveying a message of congratulations to the restaurant owner upon the excellence of his cooking.

Tripes à la mode de Caen consists of a rich and pungent mixture of tripe, calves' feet, onions, garlic, carrots, and cloves, embedded in a sandstone pie-dish and topped up with cider or white wine. The whole is then made airtight and cooked in a slow oven for seven or eight hours.

26 March 1958

[Beneath the suave surface of this act of gastronomic diplomacy there seethed a cauldron of intrigue and recriminations. The year before, on 26 August, *The Times* informed its readers that M. Jehan le Hir, President and Founder of the Caen Brotherhood of the Golden Tripe, had instituted legal proceedings against the Brotherhood itself, which had had the temerity to dismiss him as president. Denying the charge of favouritism made against him he alleged a conspiracy of jealousy and ambition among other officials of the Brotherhood.]

REBUFF FOR CONGO THE CHIMPANZEE

NEW YORK   It may be some consolation to Congo, the chimpanzee of the London Zoo, that it was only because he was not a human being that an appraiser in the United States Customs service at Baltimore refused yesterday to allow his paintings to enter this country duty-free as works of art.

'If we did not know they were produced by an animal,' the appraiser said, 'we would have thought they were good modern art. But in my opinion paint placed on canvas by a sub-human animal with no rational mind or powers of imagination does not meet our test for works of art. We have to draw the line somewhere.'

The paintings were sent from London to Dr A. R. Watson, director of the Baltimore Zoo, to be exhibited with paintings by Betsy, the celebrated chimpanzee artist of that city.

9 May 1958

[Congo's 'works' had been exhibited in September of the previous year at the London Zoo, under the auspices of Dr Desmond Morris. The reactions of art critics, as summarised in *The Times*, had in the main been appreciative, though there had been a tendency, among the more leaden-soled, to treat the affair in the spirit of the customs man.]

SEARCH FOR MODEL OF 'CHERRY RIPE'

The Royal Academy wish to contact the lady who sat for Millais's portrait 'Cherry Ripe', which is now on view there in the exhibition of Sir J. B. Robinson's collection. An advertisement in *The Times* Personal Column today states that it is believed she may have visited the exhibition recently.

Mr Henry Rushbury, Keeper of the Royal Academy, told *The Times* last night that the lady believed to have been the sitter for Cherry Ripe visited the Academy some three weeks ago. 'She came with a young man, but we failed to contact her,' he said. 'It would be of public interest if we could take a photograph of her looking at the picture. We know Bubbles; it would be nice to know Cherry Ripe also.'

8 August 1958

'WHISKY STRIKE' IN PARIS A FAILURE

The token whisky strike in Paris bars on Friday night, called as a protest over the 'Spanish champagne affair', ended in complete fiasco.

Bar-owners and barmen on the whole failed to obey the suggestion of one chain of bars that they should cease all sales of whisky to customers for one hour, as a token of French displeasure at the recent British court decision upholding the right of a wine company to describe imported white wine from Spain as 'Spanish champagne'.

The owner of a bar on the Champs Élysées commented: 'Holding a whisky strike would not have won us the battle of champagne. It would merely have upset our clients.'

15 December 1958

'She may have visited the exhibition recently...'
[SEARCH FOR MODEL OF CHERRY RIPE]

COUNTERBLAST TO BEATRIX POTTER

A warning against allowing rabbits to be confused with Flopsy, Mopsy, and Cottontail and all the other endearing rabbit characters in the Beatrix Potter stories was given at a conference of 100 rabbit clearance societies in London yesterday.

Mr J. F. H. Thomas, South Wiltshire, said: 'The rabbit has been glorified in the past: Beatrix Potter books in the nursery have meant young people growing up to think of rabbits as little darlings. We should think of doing something to put into the minds of both town and country children the idea that the rabbit is a pest.'

Mr. B. Engholm, vice-chairman of the Rabbit Clearance Advisory Council, said that the Ministry had already been asked to do what they could by educational means to correct the Flopsy, Mopsy, and Cottontail attitude. 'We are working on educational leaflets and booklets which we hope will do something to counteract it, but it is a long, hard, educational grind,' he said.

Mr. Engholm told *The Times* afterwards that the assault on childish sensibilities would be by straightforward, factual information. No attempt was being made to present the rabbit as a fictional criminal.

'Multiply Faster'

Opening the conference, Lord Waldegrave, Joint Parliamentary Secretary to the Ministry of Agriculture, Fisheries and Food, said that myxomatosis could no longer be relied upon to keep rabbits down: it was only an ally.

A contribution to a rabbit clearance society was in the nature of an insurance premium against further losses from rabbits – a premium at half price because the Ministry made a pound for pound contribution towards the cost. 'Unless these societies multiply more rapidly than the rabbit – and you know how rapidly they can multiply – the struggle against them will be indefinitely prolonged.'

Mr. P. F. Williams, south-east divisional pest officer, said that 10,000 acres could be controlled for little more than

£1,000 a year. That included a full-time exterminator paid £10 a week. One of these men had caught 95 rabbits in his first three weeks on land which members of a clearance society believed had been completely cleared by myxomatosis.

The 100 or so delegates from 26 counties decided to form a national federation of rabbit clearance societies and to set up a working party to examine the details.

6 February 1959

CAPTIVE ALBATROSS FOUND DEAD

The albatross – traditional bird of ill omen to mariners – which was brought home in the freighter Calpean Star, 15,000 tons, was found dead on board in Huskisson Dock, Liverpool, tonight.

A half sausage was found in its cage on the aft deck where it had been housed with four sea elephants, three seals, and 54 penguins brought home from Bird Island, South Georgia, by a German naturalist, Herr Erich Graeber, of Bremen, for German zoos. Mr Richard Clitherow, secretary of the Liverpool branch of the RSPCA, who met the vessel on Sunday, said tonight that he was taking the bird for an autopsy.

Earlier today nearly 60 of the 70 officers and crew of the liner staged a sit down strike on learning they were expected to take the vessel on to Oslo. Later a number of them, including Britons, Norwegians, Greeks, Spaniards, and Indians, walked off the ship. The vessel reached the Mersey on Sunday after a round voyage to South Georgia to provision the Antarctic whale fleet and bring back 5,000 tons of whale products as well as the livestock. Although some of the crew had complained at first about travelling with the albatross, a spokesman for those who walked off said tonight: 'The albatross has nothing to do with it. We had a shocking outward voyage and have had enough without going on to Norway. It means we would have to hang around Liverpool for several weeks unloading before sailing on to Norway even though our expenses home would be met by the company.'

7 July 1959

SCENTED STATIONS

After nearly two years of experiments, the Paris Métro service has now brought into effect its plans for disinfecting platforms and stations by means of a spray, mounted at the back of the trains, which on the arrival of the train in the station proceeds to spray the permanent way.

The purpose of the scheme is primarily to disinfect the stations, but travellers will notice only the agreeable smell after the departure of the train. Four lines so far have been equipped with this new apparatus, three of them suggesting the scent of the carnation, and the fourth – which incidentally passes through the Halles station, the Covent Garden and Billingsgate of Paris – a pungent smell of pine.

7 July 1959

AN HONOUR WITHOUT PROFIT

After an assistant steward on the liner *Caronia*, for the honour of his ship, had painted its name 1,500 ft up on a Norwegian mountain the ship sailed away and left him behind. He caught up with it after a chase by aircraft, bus, and steamer.

When the liner docked at Southampton yesterday, the steward, F. McNulty, aged 27, of Midanbury, Southampton, said he painted the name in white letters 600 ft above that of the liner *Andes* on the face of Merok mountain.

In hurrying down to rejoin the liner he slipped and fell 20 ft to a ledge. He waved his shirt at the *Caronia* far below in a fjord. An officer on the bridge saw him and a rescue team brought him down the mountain, but by then the *Caronia* had sailed.

McNulty said: 'I was looked after very well by the villagers at Merok, who put me on a seaplane to fly after the *Caronia*. We landed by the ship, but she was going at full speed and could not stop. Then I was flown to Maadane and made a bus and steamer trip to Bergen to catch the liner.'

A lenient view was taken of his case as it was felt he had done something for the honour of the ship. He had a day's pay stopped and the rest of the crew made a collection to cover his expenses.

7 August 1959

NO RIGHT TO STAND NEAR OWN HOME

A man who said at Thames Magistrates' Court yesterday: 'I have a right to stand near my home and get fresh air,' was told by the Magistrate, Mr Leo Gradwell: 'Curiously enough, you haven't. People always think that, but the law states you have only the right to walk up and down – not to stand there.'

Louis Goldberg, aged 53, boiler maintainer, of Wellclose Square, Stepney, E, who said he would rather go to prison than pay the fine of £2, with £1 costs, for obstructing a policeman in the execution of his duty, was allowed 14 days in which to pay.

Police constable Anthony Bell said that on Monday night in Cable Street, Stepney, Goldberg refused to 'move on' when asked to do so, and said: 'I am a British subject.'

Goldberg, who pleaded Not Guilty, was told by the Magistrate that the alternative in the case of non-payment of fine and costs would be 14 days' imprisonment. Goldberg left the Court.

19 August 1959

['Am I allowed to stand still while using a bus stop?' asked a correspondent a few days later. Towards the end of the month another man, who refused to 'move on' when asked by a policeman, was told by a Clerkenwell magistrate 'There appears to be some confusion as to what your rights really are. If you want to stand around for a bus you must stand in the proper place. It has been established that the law only gives you the right of free passage of the footpath.' Meanwhile, Mr Louis Goldberg's fine was paid by an unknown benefactor.]

TRACING THE HISTORY OF WORDS

'Bus-conductress' first appeared in print in 1952, 'clippie' came in 1941, 'bus-stop' dates from 1930, and 'bus-shelter' from 1945. These dates are the earliest in the collections of the Editor of the *Oxford English Dictionary Supplement*.

He points out in the supplement to *The Periodical*, just published, that they may well not be the right time of entry of the words into the English language. They should be regarded merely as signals or pointers. He issues an invitation, as in the past, to the public to help him with quotations and references of earlier date for these and other words needed by the compilers of the *Supplement* to the *O.E.D*.

All words and phrases in this latest batch of inquiries, alphabetically, come under B or C. 'Bubble-gum' (in the United Kingdom) starts only in 1958. 'Cocktail party' goes back to 1929. 'Clueless' (for stupid) is from 1943, 'butterflies in the stomach' from 1944. 'Business as Usual' is a veteran of 1884 – two years earlier than 'clipping' for Press cutting. But 'bummaree' (meat porter) has not been traced beyond 1955.

'Cat's Whiskers'

There are many surprises in a list which includes 'brief-case' 1936, 'brouhaha' 1945, 'brutalism' (an expressive architectural word) 1957, 'Buckley's-chance' (Australasian) 1918, 'budget' (household allowance) 1942, 'budgie' (budgerigar) 1945, 'buffet-car' 1934, 'bull' (useless routine) 1932, 'bulletin' (for wireless news) 1928, 'call-girl' (prostitute) 1952, 'cat's pyjamas' (defined as 'acme of excellence') 1930, 'cat's whiskers' 1927, 'coach' (long-distance bus) 1935, 'colour-bar' 1930, 'chestnuts' (in sense of 'pulling out of the fire') 1935, 'Chinaman' (cricket) 1937, 'chinchilla' (breed of cat) 1958, 'Churchillian' 1886, 'class-feeling' 1865, 'chain-smoking' 1930.

Old soldiers are likely to wish to fall-in with alacrity to supply the Oxford lexicographers with references to 'button-stick' earlier than 1918. 'Chelsea' should surely improve on 1923 for its bun. But few, if any, lovers of the language will have the heart to trace 'cheery-bye' farther than 1936.

4 September 1959

UNDERGROUND BAN ON 'THE KISS'

The British Transport Commission will not allow a film company to put up posters showing Rodin's statue 'The Kiss' in London Underground stations on the ground that it would 'lend itself to defacement'.

A photograph of the statue has already been used on posters all over the world to advertise the new French film *Les Amants* (The Lovers). The film, which opens today at a London cinema, has been adapted by Louis de Vilmorin, who wrote *Madame de . . .*, from an eighteenth-century story.

The film is being distributed in Britain by Mondial Films Ltd, who had planned to put up their posters at 550 London Transport sites today. Yesterday evening they heard that the British Transport Commission's commercial advertising department would not handle the poster.

Code's Provisions

A BTC official said: 'We know from experience that posters showing nude pictures, while they may be inoffensive in themselves, may attract people with nasty minds to scribble or write offensive things on them. We have a certain code of principle in these matters and one of the items in the code is that we do not accept things that would be liable to be defaced, or that are obscene or politically controversial. That does not apply to this. It is not politically controversial and it is not obscene, but it is liable to be defaced.'

29 October 1959

CALLING ALL WIZARDS

The first systematic attempt to search for signals from intelligent beings on other planets was begun last night at the National Radio Astronomy Observatory, Green Bank, West Virginia. For the next month the observatory's 85 radio telescopes will be focused alternately on two stars that might have planets able to sustain life. They are Tau Ceti and Epsilon Erindi, each about 66 million million miles from the sun. It

'. . . lends itself to defacement'
[UNDERGROUND BAN ON THE KISS]

would take radio signals 11 years to bridge the distance.

The project is known as Ozma, after the queen of the mythical land of Oz, 'a place very far away, difficult to reach and populated by strange and exotic beings', as a spokesman explained.

13 April 1960

THREE LARGE RATTLESNAKES SEEK GOOD HOME

It is not easy to shed tears of sorrow over a snake, particularly when that snake is *Crotalus terrificus*, better known as the diamond-back rattlesnake, one of the deadliest of reptiles and horrifying enough to set the flesh of even a mongoose crawling. But tears nevertheless are being shed at RAF Acklington, the home in Northumberland of No 66 Fighter Squadron – Motto 'Beware you have been warned' – who are the proud owners of three fine specimens.

From Squadron Leader Peter Pledger down to the newest recruit there will be much heartrending on 1 December when No 66 is disbanded and a new home must be found for their mascots. They may go to a zoo or there is the possibility that another squadron may take over the famed rattlesnake emblem and all that it entails.

But wherever they go, one thing is certain. They will not be handed over to youngsters such as the small boy aged 11 from South Ruislip who wrote: 'Being as I have lost my pet grass snake witch I had for a long time, do you think I could have one of your rattlesnakes if thay have the posion taken from them. My father has given me permishun to have a rattlesnake.' And then a postscript: 'We have a big garden.'

'Ole Bare Hands'

On Saturday, Battle of Britain Day, the snakes were on display to the public for the first and probably the last time under their present ownership, and it would be a pity not to record for posterity the history of their arrival in this remote corner of England. It all began some time in the autumn of 1958 with a

93

small advertisement in *The Times* asking for a rattlesnake dead or alive as a mascot. Such was the response that within weeks it looked as though the station would be overrun with reptiles.

From Nebraska a rancher wrote: 'If you haven't already gotten a rattler I can send you all you desire.' A girl in Arizona said that she all was going right out to catch one 'with her little ole bare bare hands' and send it over. A stuffed one arrived from Houston, Texas, and two more from Florida. A titled lady in the Cromwell Road, SW, sent a rattle which she had kept in a silver box for 60 years. Another entire stuffed snake arrived via Major-General Mark Bradley in Washington and a harassed BOAC executive wired to say that he had been approached by a Texan who wanted to send a live 7-ft rattle-snake – 'did the squadron really want it?'

A woman in Dallas wrote wondering where 'North Umber-land' was, and sent another stuffed snake, which she was glad to get rid of because it put her guests off their food.

Determined

About December of 1958 a rattlesnake hunter of Okeene, Oklahoma, Mr Joe Durham, sent word that he was trying to dispatch a live one but that most of the shipping agents were fighting shy. But Mr Durham was a determined man. He is the organizer of an annual rattlesnake round-up and has a society called 'The Order of the White Fang', a select club for survivors of rattlesnake bites.

He said he could send whole suitcases full of rattlesnakes, but had been delayed in doing this because some careless friends had allowed 1,000 of his snakes to escape in the small town in which he lived and he had been rather busy. Mr Durham signed his letter 'Yours with a rattle'. His enthusiasm for snakes knew no bounds and he had even devised a plan for dropping them by parachute behind the enemy lines in Korea. He enrolled the entire squadron as members of the International Association of Rattlesnake Hunters and suggested sending the officers' mess some of his canned snake fillets.

The first live rattlesnake arrived in April 1959, from a snake farm in Texas. Customs officials took one look at the label saying 'This box contains a very large Texas diamond-back rattlesnake' and wrote to ask whether it was dead or alive. When told that it was very much alive they sent it on to the squadron without further delay or examination. Unfortunately this reptile, who was given the rank of leading aircraftman and named Ponsonby Forsdyke-Smith, died soon after arrival and it was not until this summer that Mr Durham persuaded an airline to carry three more snakes.

These arrived in July and are apparently thriving in the care of Flying Officer Martin Bridge, Officer-in-charge-snakes. They have a specially built cage heated to about 75 degrees and have already shed their skins once since arrival. They are all over five feet and the largest is 6 ft 2½ in.

So far no one on the base has become eligible for 'The Order of the White Fang', but just in case serum has been sent from laboratories in Pennsylvania, who wrote saying that the best place for rattlesnakes was in a zoo.

19 September 1960

[On 12 October the snakes were sent to Jersey Zoo, in a crate labelled 'Mean creepy crawlies: for the attention of Mr Gerald Durrell.']

CHESS KING DEPOSED

BERLIN   An east German woodcarver has designed a 'socialist chess set' without a king, the anti-communist Information Bureau West has reported here. The king's place in the set, to be displayed during the chess olympics which begin in Leipzig tomorrow has been taken by a 'worker holding the economic plan in his hands'.

The rooks have become figures in the uniform of east German factory defence squads and the bishops are athletes. The pawns are workers of different trades, one carrying a hammer and another a sickle. All that is left of the original chess figures are the two knights, called 'horses' in German.

The queen remains a woman, but she is intended to depict 'the progressive intelligentsia'.

17 October 1960

EXPERTS TO TEST 'YETI SCALP'

Sir Edmund Hillary and Mr Desmond Doig, who have been on a yeti-hunting expedition in Nepal, arrived in London by air yesterday with the scalp of what is believed in Khumjung to be a yeti. With them was the scalp's guardian, Khumjo Chumbi, a village headman.

Sir Edmund said he would withhold his theories until a zoologist had examined the scalp and French and American experts had completed hair tests, but unless 'something turned up' concerning the scalp he did not believe in the existence 'of a strange new animal'.

Khumjo Chumbi, however, was in no doubt about the identity of the scalp. He said he had heard a yeti crying three times in one day, and his children had seen one.

With the scalp on a table in front of him, looking like a small leather teacosy with ginger and black bristly hairs, Sir Edmund said: 'It was in the house of a frightening old woman believed to be a witch in Khumjung. It has been in the village for 240 years and is held in respect as a good luck charm. We had a lot of trouble getting it out. The old woman said bad luck would befall the village if it left.

'Eventually we took it under three conditions: That we gave a donation to the village monastery; that one of the headmen came with us; and that we must give a donation towards a new village school. If we are not back by 5 January three Sherpas who were with us will forfeit their lands.'

'Human Head'

Khumjo Chumbi gave five low cries when asked to imitate the yeti's call. He said: 'My children saw it. They called out and it ran away. It had a human head and ran like a dog. It is about the size of a 10-year-old child.'

23 December 1960

[Following the discovery of footsteps in the snow on the Reipimu Glacier at 18,000 feet above sea level, no further trace of the yeti had been found. Sir Edmund Hillary was, however, able to borrow the scalp as described, and it was later shown to the King of Nepal. The hunt was then abandoned.]

UNFROCKING OF DR BRYN THOMAS

Dr William Bryn Thomas, former Vicar of the Church of the Ascension, Balham, was not present to hear the sentence of deposition from Holy Orders passed on him in Southwark Cathedral yesterday. At the end of the half-hour ceremony of 'unfrocking', the congregation prayed for 'our erring brother'.

The Bishop of Southwark, Dr Mervyn Stockwood, pronounced the sentence of deposition. Over five weeks ago, when Dr Thomas was found Guilty at Southwark Consistory Court of immoral conduct the Bishop deprived him of his benefice. Since then the former vicar has executed a deed of relinquishment under the 1870 Clerical Disability Act.

A simple sentence would have been enough to remove Dr Thomas's clerical status. A spokesman for the Church Information Office told *The Times* yesterday that the Bishop, by having a formal service, had 'carried the affair to its logical conclusion'.

Chancellor Attends

Half an hour before the time for the ceremony to begin there were only 20 people in the cathedral. Of these, half were reporters, and the atmosphere was soporific after the rush-hour bustle outside. A man in blue jeans slept peacefully in a pew at the front.

When the organ broke into a restrained, speculative melody, the congregation had enlarged to slightly over a hundred, including an elderly man carrying opera glasses. A score of reporters sat near the door, watching in case Dr Thomas should arrive. Photographers waited outside.

The organ gave way to the strains of the litany chanted by a procession of church dignitaries and officials. Among them, wearing his wig and a black robe, was Mr Evelyn Garth Moore, Chancellor of the diocese, who presided over the

Consistory Court. Preceded by a verger carrying his ivory-handled pastoral staff, Dr Stockwood, two Bishops Suffragan and other clergy moved into the Sanctuary.

'Office Misused'

The first lesson, read by the Bishop of Kingston from the First Book of Samuel (2: 27–35) contained the words 'for them that honour me I will honour, and they that despise me shall be lightly esteemed'. Then came Psalm 51: 'Have mercy on me, O God', followed by the second lesson from St Matthew's Gospel (7: 15–27), read by the Bishop of Woolwich. 'Beware of false prophets, which come to you in sheep's clothing, but inwardly they are ravening wolves. Ye shall know them by their fruits.'

After Psalm 130, 'Out of the depths have I cried', the Bishop of Kingston led the congregation in the Lord's Prayer, and four collects were read. The congregation stood in silence as Dr Stockwood and the Chancellor moved slowly forward to a special table just inside the chancel rails. They sat down and the Bishop, in black cassock, white surplice and scarlet hood, faced the body of the congregation and pronounced Dr Thomas's deposition from 'the office which he hath misused'.

For Archives

Dr Thomas would be 'entirely removed, deposed and degraded from . . . the offices of Priest and Deacon respectively, and we do hereby . . . remove, depose, and degrade him . . . from all clerical offices and the Orders of Priest and Deacon'.

The Bishop read the long rolling periods in a powerful voice, and momentarily it seemed that we had returned to an earlier time in the Church's history. It might have been Dr Donne eloquently and dramatically warning a seventeenth-century congregation gathered in St Paul's.

After the sentence was over, Dr Stockwood signed the documents and handed them to the Registrar, gowned and bewigged, with the words: 'Registrar, keep this in the archives of the diocese.' The Bishop then prayed that 'a true repentance

98

and amendment of life', should be granted to 'our erring brother'.

One member of the Balham Hill congregation, Mrs Olive Finbow, of Elms Crescent, Clapham, was among the congregation. Mrs Finbow, who was present at the Consistory Court, commented afterwards: 'I never thought the day would come when this evil would be wiped out. I am glad. The others could not come but I came alone. I wanted to hear the bishop pronounce the words. I cannot say I am sorry.'

Mrs Finbow added: 'I am glad this evil has been stamped on.' She said to a photographer: 'You mustn't take one of me smiling.'

Inside the church, the bishop's chaplain was explaining details of the service to reporters jostling each other by the tomb of John Gower. Only one member of the congregation was left; a young clergyman sitting at the back of the church looking up towards the stained-glass windows.

5 May 1961

BURGLARIOUS ENTRY

Elderly Mrs Janet Winn, of Hallfield Estate, Paddington, opening her diary at lunch-time yesterday, found an entry in an unknown hand: 'House burgled 5 a.m.' A burglar had stolen £24 from her wallet as she slept.

30 June 1961

'ALL THE *ILIAD*' WRITTEN BY HOMER – A COMPUTER DECIDES

With the aid of an electronic computer, Mr James McDonough, a graduate student of Columbia University, has been working on the Homeric question of how many authors were involved in the composition of the *Iliad*. He reports that the machine's conclusion, based on calculations about the metrical pattern of the poetry, is that the *Iliad* was written entirely by Homer.

Mr McDonough, who is an instructor in classics, has been working at the problem in his spare time for the past four years. For each of the 15,693 lines of the *Iliad* he has prepared a card for his computer, punched in a numerical code that indicates the metrical pattern of the line. He says that the computer, by analysing the metre, can detect differences in metric pattern and reveal stylistic mannerisms that could not normally be discovered.

The computer used was of the humble variety to be found in many offices and factories in the United States. Apart from its qualities of literary detection, which have apparently enabled it to achieve in four years what generations of scholars have unsuccessfully worked on for all their lives, the machine has a few comforting limitations: it cannot translate from the Greek, nor can it compose ionics.

7 August 1961

STALIN REGION RENAMED

MOSCOW   The name of Stalin has been removed from a street and region named after him in Minsk, capital of the Byelorussian Republic. The Supreme Soviet of the republic, by a decree dated 2 November, decided to change the name of the Stalin region to Zavodsky (factory) region, and to rename Stalin Prospekt the Lenin Prospekt, according to a copy of the republic's newspaper which reached here today. The Supreme Soviet also decided to rename the Voroshilov region in the city; it is now to be called the Soviet region.

★ ★ ★

A portrait in the foyer of the Metropole hotel in Moscow showing Lenin seated at a table reading from his works to Stalin, has been altered: it now shows Lenin sitting at the table reading to a big empty chair draped with a white dust cover.

7 November 1961

YOUTHFUL SCRIBE

This has been a notable year for the Bible. The 350th anniversary of the Authorized Version has been celebrated and a new translation of the New Testament has been published. It is doubtful, however, if any 10-year-old boy will emulate the feat of Robert Millar, of Saltcoats, Ayrshire, who, in 1872, wrote out by hand the Old Testament.

The story of Robert Millar's achievement came to light recently when I discovered among some old papers a small card which was a copy of the testimonial presented to the boy on the completion of his task.

It appears that Robert was a pupil of the Sunday School of the East United Presbyterian congregation in Saltcoats. One Sunday the minister, the Rev. George Philp, told the children about how the Bible came to be printed and of how the earliest copies had been written in long-hand. He then offered to give £1 to every boy or girl who wrote out the Old Testament within a year.

2,000 Sheets

The reverend gentleman probably thought no more of his offer, and his surprise can readily be imagined when, six months later, Robert Millar presented him with 2,000 quarto sheets of paper on which he had accomplished the task, 'punctuated generally correctly and otherwise exceedingly well executed', says the testimonial.

Describing how he copied the Bible, young Millar said that he undertook the work entirely on his own and that he had wanted to keep it a secret. 'The necessary sheets of paper, however, soon caught my mother's watchful eye. She found me out by the time I had written the first 15 chapters of Genesis. As the work was going on my father kept kindly watch over me and on several occasions turned me reluctantly into bed in the early morning.'

Naturally, even in those days, the boy's accomplishment attracted a good deal of attention. At first the news was dealt with as a noteworthy achievement on the part of the boy. A publisher in Kilmarnock offered to bind the Bible; a lady in

Dunfermline wrote asking for a carte de visite of the boy; an old lady got up a public subscription in her town and sent a small keepsake to Robert.

As the news spread it began to take a different slant and two daily newspapers criticized Mr Philp for setting so great a task and offering such a small reward. One said: 'Such tasks should be condemned and youth warned against them. Young people can know the Scriptures without writing out the text.' The other paper calculated that a lawyer would have charged £200 for a similar amount of copying and claimed that the reward would do little more than pay for the cost of the paper which the boy had used.

Stung to Action

Now Mr Philp was a very popular minister and these attacks stung his congregation to action. As the minister, on his small stipend, could not give Robert Millar a large reward, his flock decided to rally round. A public subscription was taken and, at the next annual meeting of the congregation, the lad was presented with a Bible and a purse containing 20 sovereigns.

If Master Millar wrote his own acknowledgement of these gifts it would seem that copying out the Old Testament had greatly increased his vocabulary.

In a report of the proceedings published in a local newspaper he is quoted as saying: 'The bodily and mental exercise which I daily received at school seemed always to prepare me for my task at night and give me relish for it . . . The 20 sovereigns I shall lodge in the Bank to help me over some future difficulty. This most beautiful and valuable Bible I shall strive to make my companion and guide and comforter in life. I trust my relish for its living truths shall increase as I advance in years, and then when the night of death sets in I humbly hope to go out by its blessed light to be for ever with the Lord.'

What happened to Robert Millar and his 2,000 sheets of the Old Testament? No one in his home town now seems to know.

30 December 1961

FORMER GANGSTER'S BIZARRE FUNERAL

NAPLES   A violent scuffle with photographers marked the departure this morning from a Naples parish church of an immense hearse drawn by eight black plumed horses which took the remains of 'Lucky' Luciano, one of the most notorious of the Italo-American gangsters, to a temporary resting place.

A tense atmosphere marked the whole of the bizarre funeral service. Some 300 persons were present, including former associates of the dead gangster, Italian police, members of the United States narcotics bureau taking photographs of the mourners ('just for our files', one of them said) and a host of press photographers.

Luciano's associates seemed set on trying to keep the service seemly, threatening photographers in terms familiar to the world represented among some of the mourners ('Somebody', one of them said through clenched teeth, 'is going to get hurt') and leaping at a photographer who attempted to take a picture of Luciano's brother. It was of no avail. There were not only television cameras recording the strange occasion but by the time the funeral service was in progress, with the choir intoning the solemn music of the Mass, photographers had climbed above the altar to align their flashing cameras from behind the crucifix.

Luciano was deported from the United States in 1947 and lived his last years here in Naples. He was constantly under surveillance, and was alleged to be facing arrest on narcotics charges just before he dropped dead on Friday evening.

His remains were placed today in the chapel of the English cemetery on the outskirts of Naples. According to the undertaker, arrangements are in hand for transporting them to New York, which was the scene of Luciano's activities before he went to prison in 1936.

30 January 1962

DEATH AFTER 76 YEARS IN BROADMOOR

A man sent to Broadmoor at the age of 11 for a trivial offence died there tonight, aged 87. He was Bill Giles, the longest serving patient in the institution's 99 years' history.

He was committed to Broadmoor for setting fire to a hayrick. Because of his age he spent the first five years in the female wing but at 16 he was reckoned to be old enough to mix with violent men in the male blocks.

'He got on well with everyone,' said a Broadmoor spokesman. 'He was never any trouble, and he knew the daily routine so well that he often corrected new nurses if they did not keep strictly to the timetable.'

New Suit Each Year

Every year on his birthday the authorities would send the Broadmoor tailor to block four to measure Bill for a new grey suit. He was the only patient who always got an official present. 'The other patients treated him with great respect and the staff recognized him as the most conscientious floor scrubber here. Sometimes the patients would play a trick on him and nail his bucket to the floor. But he would always take it in good part and warn them sternly. "I've been here longer than anyone, so watch it or I'll have you expelled,"' said the spokesman.

Occasionally over the years he was visited by relatives. But he outlived most of them.

8 March 1962

THE MINISTER AND THE POGO STICK

Mr Kenneth Robinson, the Labour spokesman on health matters, has detected what he assumes to be a change in the public image of the Minister of Health, Mr Powell. It is unusual for Mr Robinson, one of nature's statelier beings, to indulge in personalities. But, becoming caustic today in the Commons on the issue of nurses' pay, he allowed himself to wax scornful at the expense of Mr Powell, who had (according

'. . . bouncing around Eaton Square'
[THE MINISTER AND THE POGO STICK]

to Mr Robinson) been involved in activities unbecoming to a Greek scholar and a gentleman.

Mr Powell had been seen, he said, 'bouncing around Eaton Square on a pogo stick' at the moment when a press photographer happened by, in order to give the impression that beneath his arid exterior a human heart beat on.

28 March 1962

SEEDS BY AIR

TOKYO Hundreds of coloured balloons carrying small packets of flower seeds were released in Tokyo to float over Japan yesterday. The organizers, the 'Full of Flowers Movement', said the aim was to spread flowers throughout the country, with blooms springing up wherever a balloon lands.

23 April 1962

[During the War the Japanese devised a means of using balloons to release bombs (see p. 20 above). Fortunately for the citizens of North America, where it was hoped the balloons would descend, the scheme was a complete failure.

[Another technique with seeds was revealed in 1961: the Oxford magazine *Mesopotamia* was published with cress seeds embedded in its canvas cover. By damping the canvas the magazine could be made to sprout into life. But as we shall see on p. 134 by far the most effective means of seed dispersal in recent years has been the trouser turn-up.]

TAXI UNLIKELY TO BITE PEDESTRIANS

A taxi-driver was summoned at Plymouth Magistrates' Court today under an Act 115 years old for leaving his hackney carriage in the street without 'someone proper to take care of it'.

He was John Hockin, of Albert Road, Plymouth, and his solicitor, Mr D. B. Johnson, submitted that the summons was absurd and irrelevant in the horseless carriage era. He quoted extracts from the Act – the Town Police Clauses Act, 1847 – which empowered a policeman to remove an unattended hackney carriage with its horse or horses and harness to a livery stable near by or other place of safety and to sell the horses and harness in default of payment.

The Magistrates accepted this view and dismissed the summons and a second one for not proceeding with reasonable speed to a hackney carriage stand. Hockin was said to have left his car for 25 minutes in Union Street while he had a meal. The taxi sign was not showing.

Police Constable D. Bulley agreed in cross examination that the hackney carriage was unlikely to shy at passing traffic or to bite pedestrians.

14 June 1962

PIANO LEFT AT PARKING METER

A piano with an L plate on it was left at a parking meter in Blandford Street, Marylebone, W, last night. The parking fee was paid.

A traffic warden waited until the permitted time had expired, but no one returned to collect the piano. Later council officials removed it.

13 July 1962

[See p. 242 below for another example of a musical instrument on the road.]

FORCES TO GO ON RUBBER SOLES

I 'eard the feet on the gravel – the feet o' the
  men what drill –
An' I sez to my flutterin' 'eart-strings, I sez
  to 'em, 'Peace, be still'.

The ring of iron studs on the parade ground will be softened in a way that Kipling never foresaw when the British Army wears rubber-soled boots. For years, in various parts of the world, rubber has been tested against leather, and against leather-with-studs. Trial grounds have been used, with sharp bits of metal sticking out of the concrete and rock; and parachute troops have worn the rubber-soled boot as a regulation issue.

Now the War Office confirms that it has given the rubber trade a new specification for 'rubber soling compounds', and manufacturers will be asked to turn out an Army boot with moulded-on rubber sole. This is to be the beginning of a massive changeover in the supply of something like 250,000 pairs a year.

Ceremonial Use

Little more than the bare confirmation of these details could be learnt from the War Office this weekend, but the Federation of British Rubber and Allied Manufacturers said it was understood that the traditional Army boot would disappear, except for ceremonial drill by the Brigade of Guards. The RAF would also get the rubber sole in large quantities, and later it would spread through the Royal Navy and Royal Marines.

'All this has been in the air for a long time,' he said. 'Certain boot manufacturers make their own rubber materials and incorporate them in their product; most of the others will buy the rubber soling compounds for which the new specification has come out, and will then use the moulding process.

'But we have been given, as well, information that a subsidiary specification is being considered. This is for separately-moulded sole and heel units to be attached by adhesives to the upper – a bonding process, usually under pressure.

'This means that the trade can supply outsize shoes, of which the numbers required would not justify tooling-up for the direct moulding process.'

'Myth Dispelled'

An official statement from the federation described the experiments all over the world as having 'finally dispelled the myth that rubber soles, because they are non-porous, are somehow

108

bad for the feet'. The trade maintains that effective ventilation of a boot is not through the sole, but through the uppers, or by pumping action between uppers and ankle. A porous outer sole, it claims, can offer no advantage, provided the inside of the shoe is fairly absorptive.

The rubber soles are designed to withstand six to nine months of that wear implicit in:

> 'Boots – boots – boots – boots – movin' up an'
> down again!'

And it looks, at last, as if the pleading in that other line:

> 'Try – try – try – try – to think o' something
> different'

has been answered.

20 August 1962

HOW THE PROVOST DID IT

A writer in the American magazine *The Reporter* suggested today that a former Provost of Eton, who was said to solve the *Times* crossword while boiling his egg, committed the culinary solecism of putting the egg into cold water. 'Trials have shown that an egg may still be soft after 12 minutes of cooking in this way,' Mr J. A. Maxrone Graham wrote in a review of the crossword.

Tests by the present crossword editor of *The Times* had shown, Mr Graham said, that it was not physically possible to read out the clues and fill in the answers from the next day's issue in less than four or five minutes, and the Provost liked his egg soft-boiled.

Under the title 'The Tortuous Thunderer', Mr Graham found that one unfortunate result of addiction to crossword puzzles like *The Times*'s was that solvers tend to become intolerable punsters. He quotes a remark in a reader's letter about the egg-boiling claim: 'I say without hesitation that, while the school may have been Eton, I am quite sure the egg wasn't.'

Special Puzzle

Mr Graham respects the anonymity of *The Times* and reveals no more about the present crossword editor than that it is a woman. Beside his article he prints a sample puzzle which she composed specially for readers of *The Reporter*.

It is guaranteed to be free from cricketing terms or British abbreviations, which Mr Graham finds intimidate even the most ardent crossword devotees among his American friends. The solution is printed in the same issue.

Mr Graham reviews the history of the *Times* crossword puzzle, which has appeared daily since 1 February 1930, and he is convinced of its importance. He says: 'It has been mentioned in books, plays, and films; it has been quoted in courts of law as a standard by which to rate the intelligence of a witness; a puzzle a day has been prescribed by at least one doctor; a man was charged, and fined 9s, with a guinea costs, for cutting the crossword out of issues in a public library.'

25 September 1962

MONEY TO BURN

Three men who found after breaking open a safe in Long Island that it contained $105,000 (£37,500) in cash instead of the more modest amount they had hoped for have all been caught, because, according to the police, they became desperate in their attempts to dispose of the loot.

Some of it they spent, some they buried, some they burnt, and some they gave away. One of them went to Las Vegas and there gambled heavily in a dice game, but found that he could not lose and came away with another $10,000 in his pocket.

The police said yesterday that they finally arrested the three men after one had left a $50 note in an envelope in an hotel room. It was revealed that before doing this he had burnt $40,000, left $10,000 in a safe deposit box in San Francisco, spent $5,000 on jewelry, hidden $5,000 in his garden and another $1,500 in a shoe box under his bed.

5 November 1962

POLICE SERGEANT'S ART CRITICISM
DA VINCI WOULD BE ILLEGAL IMMIGRANT

JOHANNESBURG   A police witness at the trial of an artist accused of blasphemy told the court today he thought Picasso's paintings were ugly and monstrous and admitted he had never heard of Leonardo Da Vinci.

Detective Sergeant P. P. Pirie was giving evidence against Harold Rubin, aged 30, who is charged with blasphemy by exhibiting to the public a picture depicting Christ naked and 'with the head of an animal or some monster'.

When the trial opened yesterday, Sergeant Pirie gave evidence of receiving a warrant to seize the picture on 25 July at Johannesburg art gallery. He told the court he was a Roman Catholic and the picture had shocked him.

Today Dr G. Lowen, defending, mentioned a number of famous painters. Sergeant Pirie said he had heard of Picasso and Michelangelo but he said that so far as he was concerned Da Vinci could have been an illegal immigrant.

Christmas Hat

Sergeant Pirie praised a picture which Dr Lowen said he had taken from the top of a chocolate box, and described as ugly and monstrous two famous works of Picasso.

A Dutch Reformed Church minister, the Reverend G. A. Cruywagen, said Rubin's picture of Christ filled him with a sense of revulsion and shock.

'In the first place and purely from the artistic and aesthetic point of view, I am not inclined to call this painting a work of art. I say so because on the head is what looks like a Christmas hat. Nowhere in the Bible is it said that there was such a cap on his head.'

After reading from the Bible to show that Christ wore a crown of thorns on his head, Mr Cruywagen said the face was also revolting. 'It gives me more an impression of something animal-like,' he said.

10 January 1963

ARCHDEACON SAVES THE COUNTRY 1s

The Archdeacon of Chesterfield, the Ven. Talbot Dilworth-Harrison, has decided that to help the Government's call for national economy he will forgo the 1s annual rent the post office pays him for a telegraph pole which has stood for many years in his vicarage garden.

In his parish magazine the archdeacon says that he has received a letter from the Post Office asking him to surrender the rent. 'The document combined importunity with much delicate dealing and after a brief mental struggle I determined with abandon to renounce my rights,' he writes.

The archdeacon, who is 76, commented today: 'I do not think I ever looked at the pole. I only thought of it when the shilling came round. It seems so absurd to go to all that trouble over a shilling.'

6 February 1963

[By way of contrast, it was reported a few days later that clients were being charged 25s each for soft drinks at a Soho Club named The Red Parrot. Asked whether the club was known as a 'clip joint' the manageress said she never referred to it in these terms herself. She later went on to admit that drinks were charged for on a sliding scale – increasing by ten shillings with each consumption. When a client finally became disillusioned he was asked for a further 50s before being allowed to leave.]

THE PROPRIETIES FOR PETS

The Society for Indecency to Naked Animals picketed the White House today in an attempt to make Mrs Kennedy put clothes on her horse. One member carried a placard saying: 'Mr President, the indecency of naked animals can be cor-

112

rected through new federal laws and SINA.'

One of the three pickets outside the White House today resented the smiles of passers-by, insisting that his mission was a serious one. 'I get a bit upset with people who try to get cute,' he said.

Mr Clifford Prout, the president of the society, has explained that by mistake the wrong preposition was used in its name, which cannot now be changed for fear of losing a legacy. Claiming that the society had 50,000 members, Mr Prout also asserted that by 1969 it would be quite normal to walk down a street and see a dog in boxer shorts, or a horse in Bermudas. 'Now, of course', he added, 'there are people who dress their pets, but they do it for a status symbol. They are not thinking of the decency aspect.'

Mr Prout himself is said to have once had a baby deer which he took walking through Greenwich Village clad in shorts. 'Domestic animals share everything else with us', he is reported to have said, 'and should share our standards of propriety and decency.'

6 March 1963

WRONG NUMBERS CAUSED BY GIRAFFE

A telegraph pole at Chester zoo is to be raised about four feet – after complaints of wrong numbers. It was found that the zoo's 18-foot-tall giraffe, by stretching his neck and putting out his tongue, could grasp the wires which pass over his enclosure. Then he lets them snap back like a bow string with the result that they become entwined and calls are mixed.

Mr R Bloom, curator of mammals at the zoo, said last night: 'We have had this trouble for some time but it was only today that we noticed what the giraffe was doing.'

14 March 1963

PAINTING MACHINE

Señor Pablo Picasso, dining out in Nice last night, is reported to have announced that he had invented a painting machine. It

113

would through pressure on a keyboard apparently enable the artist to project simultaneously on to a canvas colours and forms that his inspiration had determined.

Señor Picasso is said already to have used a rudimentary version of the machine to paint some of his works. He is credited with saying that the machine could 'cut out the time lapse which the brain takes to transmit its orders to the hand'.

1 May 1963

PURRING AS A SIGN OF PLEASURE

A German scientist, it is reported, is trying to find an answer to the question why cats purr.

Your Correspondent's father, who had a 'Just So' gift for elucidating nature's mysteries, explained why cats purr to his own and his son's satisfaction. 'Satisfaction' was, indeed, the operative word.

Cats, he said, were happiest when drinking milk, and while thus engaged purred loudly to express their pleasure. Kittens, when being fed, purred even louder, at the same time kneading their mother's fur with extended and contracting claws. With mouths full of milk and nostrils buried in her fur, the purring was perhaps forced upon them by the effort to breathe through liquid, but young creatures often show the history of the race more clearly than their parents.

Cheetah Hunt

The habit of purring to express pleasure may derive from stronger drink than milk. This the writer's father first realized when, as the guest of a maharajah, he took part in a cheetah hunt in India.

The cheetah, unleashed at sight of a herd of blackbuck, had made its kill, and when the hunting party arrived was lying sprawled on its victim, drinking the life blood which poured from a severed jugular, and at the same time – of necessity perhaps – making a loud purring noise. The cheetah's claws are non-retractile, but they kneaded the blackbuck's hide.

It is a far cry to puss on the hearthrug, purring loudly and at the same time opening and shutting her claws, but this picture of feline contentment may have its origin in scenes such as that described. The domestic cat is still near its wild ancestors in habits, and even civilized man makes a purring noise when he gargles.

7 August 1963

CASTLES IN THE AIR

For several minutes today fishermen in the Gulf of Taranto saw a splendid city rise from the sea between the islands of San Pietro and San Paolo. It had, according to their reports, high buildings, towers surmounted by battlements and a long row of cypress trees. They hastened to reach it in their boats but it vanished.

Professor Parenzan, director of the Taranto institute of marine biology, explained to them that it was a mirage caused after a sudden rise in temperature, and that what they had taken to be battlemented towers were reflections of the sun's rays on the blocks of stone on the top of the dam joining the two islands.

The fishermen were apparently not persuaded. They are still convinced that they saw a city rising and then disappearing.

19 October 1963

WHAT SONGS THE BEATLES SANG

The outstanding English composers of 1963 must seem to have been John Lennon and Paul McCartney, the talented young musicians from Liverpool whose songs have been sweeping the country since last Christmas, whether performed by their own group, the Beatles, or by the numerous other teams of English troubadours that they also supply with songs.

I am not concerned here with the social phenomenon of

115

'. . . saw a splendid city arise'
[CASTLES IN THE AIR]

Beatlemania, which finds expression in handbags, balloons and other articles bearing the likenesses of the loved ones, or in the hysterical screaming of young girls whenever the Beatle Quartet performs in public; but with the musical phenomenon. For several decades, in fact since the decline of the music-hall, England has taken her popular songs from the United States, either directly or by mimicry. But the songs of Lennon and McCartney are distinctly indigenous in character, the most imaginative and inventive examples of a style that has been developing on Merseyside during the past few years. And there is a nice, rather flattering irony in the news that the Beatles have now become prime favourites in America too.

Three of Them Compose

The strength of character in pop songs seems, and quite understandably, to be determined usually by the number of composers involved; when three or four people are required to make the original tunesmith's work publicly presentable, it is unlikely to retain much individuality or to wear very well. The virtue of the Beatles' repertory is that, apparently, they do it themselves; three of the four are composers, they are versatile instrumentalists, and when they do borrow a song from another repertory, their treatment is idiosyncratic – as when Paul McCartney sings 'Till there was You' from *The Music Man*, a cool, easy, tasteful version of this ballad, quite without artificial sentimentality.

Their noisy items are the ones that arouse teenagers' excitement. Glutinous crooning is generally out of fashion these days, and even a song about 'Misery' sounds fundamentally quite cheerful; the slow, sad song about 'That Boy', which figures prominently in Beatle programmes, is expressively unusual for its lugubrious music, but harmonically it is one of their most intriguing, with its chains of pandiatonic clusters, and the sentiment is acceptable because voiced cleanly and crisply. But harmonic interest is typical of their quicker songs too, and one gets the impression that they think simultaneously of harmony and melody, so firmly are the major tonic sevenths and ninths built into their tunes, and the flat submediant key switches, so natural is the Aeolian cadence at the

117

end of 'Not a second time' (the chord progression which ends Mahler's *Song of the Earth*).

Those submediant switches from C major into A flat major, and to a lesser extent mediant ones (e.g. the octave ascent in the famous 'I want to hold your hand') are a trademark of Lennon-McCartney songs – they do not figure much in other pop repertories, or in the Beatles' arrangements of borrowed material – and show signs of becoming a mannerism. The other trademark of their compositions is a firm and purposeful bass line with a musical life of its own; how Lennon and McCartney divide their creative responsibilities I have yet to discover, but it is perhaps significant that Paul is the bass guitarist of the group. It may also be significant that George Harrison's song – 'Don't bother me' – is harmonically a good deal more primitive, though it is nicely enough presented.

Welcome Variety

I suppose it is the sheer loudness of the music that appeals to Beatle admirers (there is something to be heard even through the squeals), and many parents must have cursed the electric guitar's amplification this Christmas – how fresh and euphonious the ordinary guitars sound in the Beatles version of 'Till there was you' – but parents who are still managing to survive the decibels and, after copious repetition over several months still deriving some musical pleasure from the overhearing, do so because there is a good deal of variety – oh, so welcome in pop music – about what they sing.

The autocratric but not by any means ungrammatical attitude to tonality (closer to, say, Peter Maxwell-Davies's carols in *O Magnum Mysterium* than to Gershwin or Loewe, or even Lionel Bart); the exhilarating and often quasi-instrumental vocal duetting sometimes in scat or in falsetto, behind the melodic line; the melismas with altered vowels ('I saw her yesterday-e-ay') which have not quite become mannered, and the discreet, sometimes subtle, varieties of instrumentation – a suspicion of piano or organ, a few bars of mouth-organ obbligato, and excursion on the claves or maraccas; the translation of African Blues or American western idioms (in

'Baby, it's you, the Magyar 8/8 metre too) into tough, sensitive Merseyside.

These are some of the qualities that make one wonder with interest what the Beatles, and particularly Lennon and McCartney, will do next, and if America will spoil them or hold on to them, and if their next record will wear as well as the others. They have brought a distinctive and exhilarating flavour into a genre of music that was in danger of ceasing to be music at all.

27 December 1963

'BALL LIGHTNING' IN THE BEDROOM – OFF WITH A BANG

The rare occurrence of 'ball lightning' is reported in the current issue of the *Meteorological Magazine*. It was seen, in the form of a small, egg-shaped ball of brilliant light, in the centre of his bedroom by Mr Eric Falkner, aged 59, of Hillside Avenue, Mapperley, Nottingham, last November.

Mr Falkner said yesterday the ball spread to form a sheet of darkish green light, turned grey as it moved towards him, then disappeared with a loud bang. Mr Falkner added:

'At the time I had never heard of "ball lightning" and I had no idea what it was. I did not think of it as being an apparition or ghost of any sort because it was too vividly visible to be ghostly.

'I suppose it could have been frightening but it was all over so quickly that I did not have time to think about that.'

A Meteorological Office Official said: We cannot really explain what causes ball lightning. It is something about which we still know little, and research is still going on. It can be dangerous if it envelops a person. It is not uncommon for the "ball" to enter a room, and it has been known to "bounce".'

Our Science Correspondent writes:
Ball lightning was discussed by an international conference on atmospheric and space electricity in Montreux, Switzerland, last year. Well-attested features are said to be, first, 'a station-

119

ary bright object not particularly spherical in shape, sometimes with glowing tentacles', and, secondly, 'an illuminated path with well-defined boundaries caused by motion of the ball'.

According to a summary after the conference the glowing ball is usually four to eight inches in diameter, though some as big as 30 ft to 40 ft have been reported. It may be white, blue, red, or orange. It may vanish silently or with a bang.

It may pass close to an observer, without sensation of heat, or it may scorch wood, or even, in one case – when a ball was reported to have fallen into a water butt – bring water to the boil.

Professor P. Kapitza, the Russian scientist who worked at the Cavendish Laboratory under Rutherford, thinks ball lightning consists of plasma-gas whose atoms have parted company from most of their electrons.

8 April 1964

BOOKS THROWN AT APPEAL JUDGES

Two law books were thrown in the direction of Lord Denning, Master of the Rolls, in the Court of Appeal yesterday, after the Court had dismissed an application by a woman litigant who appeared in person.

Miss Vera Beth Stone, aged 37, heard the Court – Lord Denning and Lords Justices Harman and Diplock – dismiss her *ex-parte* application for leave to appeal against a decision on a review of taxation.

Then she picked up two books and threw them towards Lord Denning, saying that it was not a personal matter but that she hoped by this means to bring her complaint before the Court.

The books – copies of *Butterworth's Workmen's Compensation Cases* – taken by her from the Court library, passed between Lord Denning and Lord Justice Diplock, Miss Stone saying that it did not have to be tomatoes.

She was restrained as she picked up a third book, remarking that she was running out of ammunition.

After Lord Denning had asked her if she would leave the Court, she said that she would only come back and throw some more books, and that she wanted to be committed for contempt of Court.

Lord Denning sent for the tipstaff and when he arrived told him to remove Miss Stone from the Court, and see that she did not return.

As Miss Stone left the Court with the tipstaff, she said to Lord Denning: 'May I congratulate your Lordship on your coolness under fire?'

16 June 1964

'DO NOT LET TOPLESS DRESSES SHOCK US'

The Archbishop of Canterbury, Dr Ramsey, today gave his opinion on topless dresses and other modern fashions. He thought it was the worst thing possible for church people to adopt an attitude of being shocked.

'We must just accept the fact that young people express themselves in new methods of dress that may seem queer to the older of us,' he said at a press conference here. 'We must accept the fact and get alongside them and understand them.'

Asked if a person who was offended by a topless dress should express his disgust Dr Ramsey said: 'A Christian should express his disgust at anything indecent, but short of that the less disapproval he expresses the better.'

He added: 'This is all tied up with the approach of the Church to secularism. Many people are just not interested in God or religion. Christian people must get alongside them and get as interested as possible in those people's conversation, outlook and ideas.'

1 July 1964

[The day before, the Guild of Lady Drivers had also issued a statement on topless dresses, which it held to be uncomfortable, impractical and dangerous – a distraction to other road users that could cause accidents. One

121

may readily imagine the hazardous consequences of following too literally the Archbishop's advice to 'get alongside' the topless female driver.]

A FEW ODDITIES OF THE BANKING WORLD

Unnoticed amid the thunder of great events, certain private habits began to change, half a century ago. One of them I have seldom heard remarked, though it was significant and lasting. The little chain purses in which men kept their chinking sovereigns began to be put away, as the coins themselves disappeared from circulation, and the practice began of using leather pocket-books, to hold the new pound notes. Paper tokens of this kind had not been in use in England since the far-off days of George III.

I was conscious of such things because I was in the habit of noticing what my father wore and used, and he was one of the first to change. At that time, and for many years to come, he was chief cashier at the Lombard Street office of one of the oldest private banks in the world.

As he seemed to absorb history and lore of all kinds as naturally as he breathed, I learnt a good deal about day-to-day financial dealings. For instance, there was the odd expression by which bankers used to refer to the sum of £1 1s 1d. This was called a 'Nelson'. Asked why, my father replied, as if it was the most natural thing in the world: 'Why Nelson? Oh, one eye, one arm, one love.'

A Lightning Eye

Taking in a large amount of coin of the realm during the course of each week, my father acquired a lightning eye and a ready touch as a guard against spurious stuff. Once or twice he was had but not often. I have before me at this moment two half-crowns which diddled him, as they would have done most experts. They bear the head of the young Victoria. One of them has a date which looks like 1877, but it is too faint to be sure. The other is 11 years earlier, of a date when no half-crowns were minted.

The curiosity about these coins is not merely that they are deceptive, but that they look as if they had circulated for years and years before being spotted. Perhaps they had. They are so worn that they would come within the classification 'fair' or even 'poor' in a numismatic catalogue, and 'poor' is usually very rubbed indeed. They have both been slashed in three places, and will never deceive again. But a craftsman made them.

My father inherited a story of another sort of fraud which goes back to the reign of William IV. It may be worth preservation as an idiosyncrasy of an extremely rich man. Every Friday morning, so one of my father's predecessors told him, one of the wealthier dukes, at a time when most dukes were fabulously well-endowed, used to call at the bank for a bag of 50 sovereigns. This would be ready for him, carefully counted.

Weekly Pantomime

Every week the same pantomime would be gone through. The bag would be handed over, and the duke would check the coins. At the end, he would raise his eyebrows at the cashier and say: 'There seems to be some mistake: one of these coins is a new farthing.' 'Oh, your grace,' the cashier would answer, '*what* an unfortunate error, and what a good thing you checked over the coins to make sure they were right.' The farthing – it was a farthing right enough each week – would be handed over, and another sovereign slipped across the counter for the bag.

Everyone at the bank had at one time or another covertly watched the duke produce the farthing from the waistcoat pocket into which he duly slipped a sovereign, and had chuckled to themselves at the seraphic look on his face as he walked away, convinced that he had 'done' the bank again.

I asked my father why the little game had never been exposed, why the bank meekly bore the loss each Friday of 19s 11¾d. 'No point', he explained, 'in losing a customer who kept £100,000 on current account.' The logic was unanswerable.

123

A Reminder

The odd thing is that although the William IV farthing is the same diameter as the sovereign, one has a milled edge and the other has not, and there is little real possibility of confusing them, for the reverse of the sovereign has a coat-of-arms, while the farthing has the familiar representation of Britannia. Although there is no one alive who remembers what colour a William IV copper coin was, when fresh from the Mint it would have been much duller than gold.

I still keep a sovereign or two to remind me what people kept in their chain purses when I was a boy, but to try to recall how much each one could then have bought, in the way of sweets or toys, takes one into legendary realms. The sovereigns themselves get a fraction more valuable year by year, which is more than anyone would dare to say of the contents of a current pocket-book.

18 August 1964

CASANOVA LETTER FOUND IN CASTLE

PRAGUE   A letter purporting to be an autobiography of the eighteenth-century Italian adventurer, Giovanni Casanova, has been found with other documents on Casanova at a castle in northern Bohemia, the Czechoslovak news agency, Ceteka, said tonight.

'My mother brought me into the world at Easter on 2 April 1715. The day before this she had had a great longing for lobster. I like lobster too,' says the letter, uncovered after 176 years at Duchcov castle, where Casanova was librarian and where he died in 1798. Written eight months before Casanova's death, the letter goes on: 'At the age of 21, I was adopted as son by one of the many wealthy Venetian powers and, being of hardy means, journeyed through Italy, France, Germany, and Vienna. I sought my luck in Berlin and Petrograd, but found it in Warsaw in 1765.

'Nine months later, I lost it because I engaged in a duel with General Bramicky. I shot him in the stomach but in three months he was recovered – and I was very glad.' In 1783, he had set out for Berlin, but met a Count Waldstein who took him to Duchcov. 'This is the only history of my life that I have ever written and I permit anyone, anywhere, to use it. *Non erubesco evangelium.* (This true story does not make me blush.) Giovanni Casanova, 17 September 1797.'

9 November 1964

TIGRESS AS SECURITY FOR BANK LOAN

A woman animal trainer at Detroit, Michigan, has obtained a loan of $1,000 (£357) from a bank with a tigress as collateral. The transaction was concluded promptly, for she brought the tigress with her. The animal, named Tinker Bell, was only a little one, weighing 25 lb.

The trainer told the bank people that she operated an animal rental agency and there was a great demand for tigers now. She said Tinker Bell would have life insurance, underwritten by Lloyd's of London, and the loan would be repayable from rental payments for the animal.

11 December 1964

CAFÉ ROYAL CASTS A LOOK BEHIND

With a hundred reeking, ormolu candles, with a raw fanfare of gladiatorial trumpets, and with self-conscious, *fin de siècle* nostalgia the Café Royal in Regent Street, W, yesterday celebrated its hundredth anniversary.

A hansom cab clattered through clogged traffic to the door. Waiters in Victorian smocks smirked. A cake ornate with pictures of Toulouse-Lautrec henchmen in long aprons was reverently sliced. Magnums of champagne popped ostentatiously. A froth of cinema and television people circulated, trying to look like something out of *The Yellow Book*.

A 'period' string quartet in mutton-chop whiskers with soulful side-glances played 'The Blue Danube'. Every male guest was issued with a melancholy, wilting, green carnation. There were marble-topped tables, gilt and red plush chairs, palms and ferns, and Napoleonic trophies. The public relations consultants reassured the assembly that 'many titled people and several millionaires' were present.

Illustrious Roll

The list of Café Royal customers since 11 February 1865 rings like a roll call at school on a hot summer evening long ago – Beardsley, Beerbohm, Bottomley... Caruso, Chesterton, Dickens, Diaghilev... Wells, Whistler, Edgar Wallace. Yesterday's pygmies strutted and fretted their hour upon the stage, trying to stand as high as the congregation of illustrious ghosts.

Whatever would Oscar have thought of it all? It all seemed slightly different from the days when a marble-topped table and wine at the Café Royal cost 2s for the evening. He would certainly have approved of the rivers of free 'bubbly'. He would have noted with interest the presence of Lord Queensberry. But he would probably have reflected that the Lyons (or at any rate the Charles Forte) and the lounge lizard keep the courts where Oscar gloried and drank deep.

12 February 1965

MINOAN SCRIPT DISCOVERY

A Mycenaean studies conference at Cambridge has received a sensational report which supports the correctness of the decipherment of the Minoan Linear Script B by the late Michael Ventris 13 years ago.

It came from a young Belgian scholar, M. Jean-Pierre Olivier, who for the past three months has been studying clay tablets in the museum at Iraklion in Crete.

He told the conference that he had discovered among the objects found in the excavations conducted at Knossos by Sir Arthur Evans at the beginning of the century, but never before published, a clay sealing, a kind of label often used by the Mycenaean Greeks. On one side was a strange rectangular object, the identity of which could not be guessed, but another side provided the description in the Linear B script.

It reads *A-sa-mi-to*, which is plainly the rare Homeric word *asaminthos*, long known to be a borrowing from some earlier language of the Aegean and meaning bathtub.

12 April 1965

AIRBORNE CATS LOSE A BATTLE

KUALA LUMPUR   The Australian Army has suffered its first defeat of the Borneo border war. Five cats that had been dropped from the air to clear a forward post of rats, have died after fierce battles in which they were outsized and outnumbered by the rats. A Kuching newspaper has suggested the use of pythons instead, but it remains to be seen whether the Australians will prefer snakes to cats, even if they win.

22 April 1965

WHITE HOUSE CALLS WENT ASTRAY

President Johnson today thanked a New York housewife for

her diplomatic handling of telephone calls for the White House that came to her by mistake.

'I couldn't be more gratified to know that you are handling these calls with all the diplomacy of an ambassador and the warmth of an understanding woman,' the President wrote to Mrs Rose Brown of Glendale, in the New York suburb of Queens.

Mrs Brown's telephone number is exactly the same as that of the White House. To complicate matters further, the area codes for long-distance dialling are almost identical, 202 for Washington and 212 for New York.

In receiving the calls meant for the White House, Mrs Brown has always been polite to the sometimes distinguished caller. Mr Johnson promised in his letter to be just as careful in receiving telephone calls that are meant for the Brown family.

1 May 1965

YOUR MONEY OR YOUR LIFE IN YORK

A link between widely differing postal advertising campaigns has made it appear that the Archbishop of York, Dr Coggan, is advertising a race meeting.

For several months Dr Coggan has been leading an 'Opportunity Unlimited' campaign in his diocese to encourage church workers to go out and meet people in other walks of life. To promote the campaign a printed sticker is being attached to church correspondence.

At the same time York race committee has been paying to have all letters leaving York stamped with the dates of the May meeting. So many envelopes are going out marked 'Opportunity Unlimited. York Races May 18, 19, and 20.'

Major Leslie Petch, manager and clerk of the course at York, said today: 'People have been contacting me from all parts of the county pointing out the mixup. It is all very amusing – and good advertising.'

The Post Office at York said: 'We cannot control what stickers people put on their envelopes. And all mail going out of York at the moment has the races stamp on it. It is perhaps a bit unfortunate, but we do not think anyone is very upset.'

Dr Coggan, who is said to be 'highly amused' by the coincidence, issued a statement which read: 'There is opportunity unlimited to lose money at York races. There is opportunity unlimited to win life in this diocesan movement. As Dick Turpin often said on his way to York, it is a case of your money or your life.'

11 May 1965

DICKENS'S WATERFALL SHOWERBATH

The waterfall that Dickens had converted into a showerbath still drops noisily down the cliff at Bonchurch in the Isle of Wight. Nobody bathes in it today, but an occasional holidaymaker dips in a toe and reports the cascade icy cold. The novelist, who sluiced himself each morning, was, it would seem, something of a Spartan.

Dickens went to Bonchurch, just outside Ventnor, in July 1849, hoping that the exchange of London air for sea breezes would help him to compose the fifth number of *David Copperfield*, which was giving him trouble. He fell in love with a house called Winterbourne, now an excellent hotel, and on the night of the 16th was writing ecstatically about it to his wife back in Devonshire Terrace. A postscript mentioned 'a waterfall in the grounds, which I have arranged with a carpenter to convert into a perpetual showerbath'.

Taller Story

Two local builders, Messrs Jolliffe and Day, who had put up most of the Bonchurch villas, including Winterbourne, were commissioned to harness the waterfall. Their construction took the form of a large wooden tub with holes in the bottom, and a wooden hut in which the bather was hidden during his ablutions.

The project plainly touched Dickens's imagination, for in a letter on 18 July he was gleefully telling a friend about the stupendous task he had set the carpenters in converting the '150 ft waterfall'. Ten days later, in a letter to his publisher, he again referred to it, but by that time the height of the waterfall had grown to 500 ft.

On a small seaside community locked away on the southern side of the island 120 years ago (Dickens wrote that the journey by train over the 75 miles from Waterloo to Portsmouth took four hours; then there was the boat trip and a further 10 miles by road) the effect of all this strange activity near the beach may be imagined.

Dickens himself touched on it in his letter to the publisher Bradbury. 'We have made all visitors in search of the picturesque mad, by putting up an immense wooden caravan on the beach to shut in a noble waterfall with some 500 feet of fall, which we take every morning, to the unbounded astonishment of the aboriginal inhabitants.'

On top of this, the natives had to accustom themselves to Dickens's morning walks up to St Boniface Down, a height of 770 ft above sea level, from Winterbourne, which stands at 150 ft and, later in his stay, his staggering from one side to the other of the local roads as he walked – due, he professed, to some peculiarity which he discovered in the climate of the undercliff.

The writer's curious infatuation with his waterfall showerbath reached a far wider public as the summer of 1849 went on. Living nearby at Bonchurch was the *Punch* contributor John Leech, and on 8 September, about a month before Dickens finally left the island, he preserved for all time in that journal the early morning ritual with a cartoon supposedly based on an actual incident.

Headed 'Domestic Bliss', and mentioning no names, it shows a scowling man, generally accepted as Dickens, peering from behind a curtain across a shower cubicle. He wears a tall conical hat like a dunce's cap to keep his hair dry, and water drips from his face. Outside is a maid-servant. 'If you please, sir, here's the butcher,' she is saying. 'Missus says, what will you have for dinner today?'

Standing in 1940

Like everybody else in the middle of the last century, butchers no doubt had more time, which was probably as well, as the

'If you please, sir, here's the butcher . . .'
[DICKENS'S WATERFALL SHOWERBATH]

maid, to put her query about the menu, would have had a round trip of a quarter of a mile or more down the rough 150 ft to the beach and back again. It is difficult today to trace the exact route which she would have taken, for the original garden is now shared by several houses.

Dickens's waterfall tumbles down prettily through one of them, disappears underneath a public footpath, then drops almost vertically through a second before being directed through a pipe beneath a rough shore road into the sea.

Jolliffe and Day did their work well, for their wooden shower contraption was still standing strongly in 1940, when it was dismantled. Whether his regular resort to it helped Dickens clear his head for the composition which he found so hard in town is not recorded, but it may be significant that writing until 2 o'clock each afternoon in a first-floor room overlooking the Channel he completed not only the difficult fifth number of *David Copperfield* but the sixth as well.

24 June 1965

'FIRST DESIGNER OF SWINGING WING' CLAIM

Managing an antique shop here selling bric-à-brac to the tourists – 'my little summer holiday job' – is a man who might have revolutionized international aviation 15 years before its time. Mr Leonard Baynes claims to have been the first designer in the world to patent the variable geometry or swinging wing aircraft, which if it had been taken up would have given Britain a long lead in this field.

He spoke in the shop today of the United States F111 fighter, which can fold back its wings in supersonic flight and then spread them wide for low-speed landings, and said: 'It may well be that the Americans incorporated some of my ideas in their machine.'

'Nothing Happened'

It was in 1949, Mr Baynes said, that he completed and patented the design of the Baynes variable sweep fighter. It was a breathtaking concept for that period. Powered by two Rolls-Royce jets, it was to fly at up to 1,000 m.p.h. with wings folded, but land on the deck of an aircraft carrier at only 100 m.p.h. with wings outstretched.

'I sent all the plans to the Ministry of Supply,' he said. 'They classified them top secret and stopped me reading a paper on the project to the Royal Aeronautical Society. Nothing happened. I kept chasing them but it just fizzled out.' He smiled wryly and went on: 'Some years later I bumped into a high official at the Ministry, who said: "Oh hello, Baynes. What a pity you dropped your variable sweep idea."'

The patents which he took out in Britain in 1949 have now run out but others in America and Canada still exist. With the resurgence of interest in the swinging wing, Mr Baynes is hopeful that he may yet salvage something from his plans of 16 years ago.

Different Concept

The variable wing was no sudden flash of inspiration, he said. He had been designing aircraft for many years before the war, including work on the Short flying boats and the world's first glider with an engine that retracted once the machine was high enough to soar.

Had he worked with Dr Barnes Wallis, generally considered the 'father' of variable geometry? Mr Baynes replied: 'No. He was working along a different concept altogether and came to his conclusions later than I did.'

Mr Baynes's claim has been borne out by an authority on aviation history. Writing in an aviation supplement of *The Times* recently, Major Oliver Stewart said: 'To him belongs the credit for seizing upon the essentials of comprehensive, inflight variable sweep... Looking through his patents one finds it hard to understand how the scientists and technical experts could have been so wrong.'

2 July 1965

[Sir Barnes Wallis's major paper on swing-wing aircraft, 'The Application of the Aerodynamics of Three Dimensional Bodies to the Stabilisation and Control of Aerodynes', was published in 1946. His prototype swing-wing model, Wild Goose, first flew on 19 January 1950.]

THE GREAT TRAIN ROBBERY HOAX

Mr Boris Belitsky, a commentator for Moscow radio, following up Moscow's radio campaign on the Great Train Robbery of 1963, said it was an 'enormous hoax played on the British public' by the British Secret Service. The 'quite conclusive evidence' he had promised to give was based on indiscretions of a British civil servant whom 'it is possibly best not to name' and a series of strange coincidences.

Mr Belitsky said the Secret Service organized the robbery of the mail train because it feared the Labour Party would cut its expenditure. Scotland Yard and the prison authorities had also cooperated with the robbers.

The commentator, recalling that after the robbery the gang hid in a deserted farmhouse, alleged that the police took no action on a tip that there were signs of activity there until 24 hours later. By that time the gang had fled with the money. 'The fact that they had been warned of Scotland Yard's intentions was obvious,' he said.

Mr Belitsky added that the police had been 'quite pleased with themselves, confident of making more arrests but rather less confident of recovering the money'. It was a hoax that cost £2,500,000.

20 October 1965

WEEDS KNOW NO FRONTIERS

Weeds are determined travellers, ready to steal a lift if they have no transport of their own like the willowherb's seed parachutes. As likely as not when I stepped from a Comet at Nicosia last year I had shepherd's purse seeds in the mud of my shoe instep, for this plant grows profusely near my garden gate in Surrey.

A close check by airport officials (they even took a half-eaten apple from a child for fear of importing disease) can hardly stop this sort of invasion by weeds.

So a common English plant can hop 2,000 miles between dawn and dusk, just as – although far more slowly – many of our weeds sailed to North America with the early emigrants and today cause no end of trouble. Couch grass, convolvulus, fool's parsley, groundsel, fat-hen, thistle, all got there.

The faster tempo of modern life is, of course, speeding the spread of plants from country to country, and often man is the unwitting carrier. I once sowed fluff from my trouser turnups and raised some fine alyssum plants which turned out to be the pale, compact form *citrinum* – a relic from a visit to a famous rock garden at seeding time.

Sir Edward Salisbury did much better: he raised 300 plants from one sample of trouser turnup 'dust', and sweepings from church pews yielded plantain, daisy, pearl-wort, chickweed, and an assortment of grasses.

Down the Drain

There are new factors at work. 'Food for the wild birds' sold in proprietary packets is leading to the occurrence of many alien plants, through being scattered in gardens and parks or perhaps carried by birds to a neighbouring county. This doubtless explains salvia, centaurea, and other aliens popping up in unexpected spots, Buckingham Palace grounds among them.

The growing popularity of the home aquarium is also playing its part. Whenever a tank is turned out for cleaning, water plants may find their way into ditches and drains. After all, Canadian pondweed, which finally choked waterways in Britain, is supposed to have begun its disastrous career when a scrap went down the plughole of a laboratory worker's basin.

Most alien plants fail to stand up to the competition of the native herbage and soon disappear, but not all. The pineapple weed from Oregon can now be found on waste land through-out England, scenting the breeze with its fruity smell when bruised underfoot; and the story of the Himalayan balsam is not yet ended. In my time it has spread down the river Aire almost to the centre of Leeds; it thrives along the fouled

Thames and on the Exe, Tweed, and other rivers. Its explosive pods hurl seeds out on to the river's current: this invader needs no muddy shoe, with Comet, to get around.

25 January 1966

MUSEUM WELCOMES COURTING COUPLES

A city's museum welcomes courting couples who are paying a 6d entrance fee for the privilege of 'necking' in the museum's dimly lit 'bird room'. It is happening in the Norwich Castle Museum, with the blessing of the curator, Mr Francis Cheetham, aged 37.

He said today: 'It is one of our jobs to provide a public service. We ought to be proud that we are providing a quiet, warm room, out of the rain, for courting couples. They are some of our best behaved visitors. They have no time for vandalism. We often find that after a time they actually become interested in the exhibits.'

Couples go to the museum to snuggle in the corners of the Norfolk Room, which displays wild animals and birds of the East Anglian countryside in their natural surroundings. Mr Cheetham commented: 'I think the couples pick the room because it is just like being in the countryside, but in the dry. They marry and then bring their children along to see the birds.'

10 March 1966

WHEN GREEK ATHLETES GAVE UP WEARING SHORTS

Snow swallowed up the Classical Association in Cardiff today. Delegates cancelled their afternoon sightseeing excursions, brought forward tomorrow's lecture to today, and in a piece of classical irony, just to rub things in, they spent the afternoon looking at pictures of ancient athletes exercising their bronzed bodies under the strong sun of Greece.

Professor H. A. Harris, of St David's, Lampeter, examined the evidence on vase paintings and sculptures for what actually went on at an ancient athletics meeting. The sporting journalists of the time were a bit vague about the events themselves, and concentrated on purple passages of eulogy.

So we have to turn to pictures to answer such puzzling questions as when Greek athletes gave up wearing shorts. It all seems to have been an accident, like the invention of Rugby – one day a runner lost his shorts halfway down the track, and subsequent sprinters stripped and never looked back.

Musical Aids?

The two conundrums in the running events are the starting gate and the turn around the post in longer races. The vases never show a starting gate. But they do offer lots of runners frozen on their marks in a position which suggests that they started when a bar in front of them dropped.

Were the ancient discus throwers a lot of chuckers who bent the throwing arm and would have been no-balled by any cricket umpire? The vases suggest that they were. Professor Harris wonders whether a modern discus thrower might not get some extra length by imitating them.

The pictures may also solve the riddle of why anyone would ever want to throw a stupid-shaped object like a discus. It may originally have been an ingot of metal which the winner kept as his prize. And who is this mysterious flute player who tootles away beside the performers in all the field events? Can he be there to assist their rhythm? Would the Beatles help our Olympic Games squad?

The vases also show that boxers wore scrum caps, and wristbands as at Wimbledon to wipe the sweat off their foreheads. An ambitious runner uses a hare to pace him. Long-jumpers in mid-air swing weights to give momentum. A wrestler gouges at an eye and his opponent appeals for a foul. A girl gold medallist clutches her skirt and hurtles round a vase, looking over her shoulder to see how far behind trail her opponents. The rule book for all these ancient sports is preserved only on the paintings.

15 April 1966

'ALICE' HEDGEHOGS TO BE 'OFFICIAL'

The BBC have accepted an offer, from an 'official source', of 15 or 16 hedgehogs to be used in the croquet scene of their film of *Alice in Wonderland*.

The Royal Society for the Prevention of Cruelty to Animals have been inundated with protests from animal lovers since the BBC's appeal for hedgehogs. Many feared they were to be used as croquet balls.

The film sequence, using the 15 'official' hedgehogs, will be made at Albury Park, near Guildford, this week. The BBC emphasize that they will not be hit through croquet hoops; stuffed toy hedgehogs are to be used for this.

23 June 1966

[On 24 November the BBC announced that the film produced by Dr Jonathan Miller, was unsuitable for children. 'In the past 100 years we have thought of Alice as a charming fairy story. But there is an enduring melancholy which outlasts the fun. It reveals the silent fears of growing up.']

CLAIM ON FIRST MAN-POWERED FLIGHT

A new claim has just been suggested to us for the £5,000 prize still going begging, for the first man-powered flight. One R. Anderson claimed to have flown in 1887 when he found himself stranded in Zanzibar, where he had gone hoping to link up with Stanley.

His story was that he got some long bamboos with great leaves and tied them with grasses into the shape of a light platform. On two sides of it he added a fan-shaped wing, extending from the centre about 30 ft.

He made each wing by running out bamboos and then stretching broad leaves across them. He added paddles to steer the concern and make progress.

'In the Air All Night'

To get airborne he made Africans tow his machine at a brisk gallop at the end of a rope. 'Immediately I soared', he wrote, he jerked the rope from their hands and began paddling. He stated that he 'remained in the air all night'. Next day the wind fell.

'My machine came lower and lower until it came into contact with some trees and began to break up; and I came to the ground, without injury. In 18 hours I had travelled upon the air some 100 miles.'

He ended firmly: 'No, it's no use saying that flying can't be done, because I've done it.'

Expert's Opinion

Anderson showed his interviewer plans and drawings, which he had placed before the Royal Geographical Society, hoping for its aid in helping him to reach the North Pole 'in a very original manner'. It seems the RGS was not playing.

We asked Mr Charles Gibbs-Smith, the authority on the history of flying, what he thought of this story, unearthed from the files of *Cassell's Saturday Journal* of 4 January 1893. He says it is new to him and of serious interest to students of forerunners of the aeroplane.

14 December 1966

CURRY GAVE HER A PINK TOUCH

Everything a girl touched turned bright pink after she ate a curry in a restaurant. Her blouse and skirt took on a tinge of pink as she carried out her duties as a shorthand-typist at the Darlington factory of Chrysler-Cummins Ltd. Letters she typed turned pink and patches appeared on her desk and chair.

Dr Valentine Crowley, doctor at the factory, investigated and after four days of laboratory tests he found that a spice in the curry had produced a form of pink dye through her pores.

11 January 1967

'Then I shall start shooting . . .'
[ONE MAN TAKES ON THE LUFTWAFFE]

ONE MAN TAKES ON THE LUFTWAFFE, CATAPULT AT THE READY

MUNICH   A German who threatened to shoot down west German Starfighters with his home-made catapult if they flew too low over his house, claims he has won his first victory.

Herr Helmut Winter, aged 48, who declared war on the Air Force this week because he said its aircraft flew only 500 ft above his house, stated today that the aircraft had since returned to the regulation minimum of 2,300 ft.

But his giant catapult, constructed on the lines of a drawing by Leonardo da Vinci, is ready to be moved into his back garden near a heap of half-bricks and stones, oiled ready for action.

'I expect within a week or 10 days they will be back down to 500 ft again; then I will start shooting,' he said patting his war machine.

Herr Winter was an artillery observer in the war, 'But I have nothing against aeroplanes themselves,' he said. He has had a call from Dr Manfred Schreiber, the Munich police chief, 'who does not seem to know whether I am serious or not. He should keep those fighters away unless he wants to find out.'

The catapult is mounted on a base 6 ft long by 4 ft wide and its 6 ft wide bow of wood and metal springs is strung with wide strips of strong rubber to fire projectiles. The rubber is drawn into the firing position by a lever.

18 February 1967

DEATH WAITS FOR NAPLES HEARSE

Police are today investigating a fusillade which shattered the windows of one of the finest hearses in Naples, frightening not only the six black-plumed horses but also the undertaker's coachman, who fled across the fields in his long black coat and top hat.

The incident occurred at Casal di Principe, north of Naples. The funeral was that of a rich man whose four children wanted to see him buried in spendour. They approached a number of undertakers and chose a Neapolitan firm which had the most impressive coach and staff.

The funeral apparently passed off without incident, but as the coachman set off on the return to Naples in the twilight he saw lights from behind a hedge and heard the shots which smashed the windows of the hearse.

Though he did not wait to meet the assailants, others guessed that they were employed by a rival firm of undertakers angry at somebody else's hearse being active in what they regarded as their territory.

4 March 1967

SHY, TIMID SNAKES NEED OUR CARE

Beware of snakes, but in the sense of a notice 'Beware of lambs' seen recently, do so to avoid harming them. Snakes lie out on sandy tracks across the heather, basking in the sun.

Almost certainly adders or vipers, they are shy, timid creatures, more frightened of us than we should be of them. Given time, they will have slithered safely out of sight before we reach the spot.

The 'deaf adder' is not deaf, but when sunbathing on a sandy footpath it is probably warned by vibration rather than by sound that someone is coming.

Adders are more likely to be taken by surprise when coiled in the heather, or in a clearing among the bracken, but even then there is no danger if one allows the reptile to uncoil and glide quietly away. A hand too hastily extended might be bitten, but the adder will not attack unless it is cornered or is trodden on.

Most dogs have a healthy regard for snakes, and will do no more than bark at them, having an inborn fear of the hiss. Our English springer, Fleck, has on several occasions tried to save my life, jumping up in an effort to knock the medicine glass from my hand, thinking the sound made by the dissolving tablets was the hissing of a snake! The hiss, however, usually means the snake is frightened, and wishes only to be left alone.

On the chalk downs in Surrey a favourite sunbathing haunt

of adders in spring is along the sheltered, sunny side of the woods that crown the hills. Every yard or so one hears the rustle of snakes disappearing into the undergrowth. I have often hastened their departure with my walking stick, but the adder stirred gently in this manner has merely turned its head and hissed in protest, then continued on its way.

Picnicking at Leith Hill, among the pines, my wife and I once found ourselves in what could only be described as a colony of adders. At least half a dozen were sheltering, like us, from the noonday sun.

An unusually pale specimen, creamy, almost milk-white in colour and showing the black zigzag markings distinctly, tried to escape by climbing the nearest pine tree, but fell back again and again. I thought it my duty to warn a party of girl hikers, who, far from being alarmed, crowded round in great excitement.

I have never had to kill an adder or viper, though obviously this may sometimes be necessary. In cases of snakebite, fortunately rare, a ligature should temporarily be applied (a shoe lace will do) and the wound, if accessible, should be sucked until medical attention can be obtained.

22 May 1967

[The writer of this article was evidently unimpressed by another article published a few months earlier in which the dangers of ligatures in cases of snakebite are explained, and the myth of 'sucking out the poison' is exposed. Injuries resulting from snakebite, as the author of this piece explained, are generally due to the necrosis of limbs too tightly bound, or to infection of the wound. The snake venom itself, in Europe at any rate, is not a medical problem.]

THE MONARCH FROM N1

World leaders, Israelis and Arabs pondering over the intractable problem of Jerusalem's future need ponder no longer. Dr Aris Shevki de Lusignan, who at present lives in Islington, has a suggestion of beautiful simplicity; that he should take his rightful place as king of a (neutral) Jerusalem.

Dr de Lusignan claims to be the last descendant of the royal house of Lusignan and of James de Lusignan, who in the early sixteenth century was king both of Cyprus and Armenia as well as of Jerusalem. He believes that, with a king to lead them, the citizens of Jerusalem will have a sense of belonging, a national pride that will transcend all racial prejudices.

Coupled with his accession to the Holy City's throne he requires that Jerusalem should become an international city for Jews, Christians and Muslims alike.

'The success of the integration of all the different communities in Jerusalem will lead to similar arrangements to cover the whole of the Middle East,' he says.

Castle or Tent

Dr de Lusignan, who plans to take the title Prince Guy de Lusignan of Jerusalem, is convinced that the Holy City would welcome 'the return of their Prince'. He even suggests a plebiscite, organized by the United Nations, to prove it.

Once established there, he would set up a committee with representatives from all religions and interested countries. This, he says, would be responsible for the internal politics of the city. Foreign affairs would be in the hands of the United Nations.

'I don't mind where I live,' he said modestly. 'I'm not interested in personal ambition. I'll find a castle or a tent to settle myself.'

His kingdom will not be short of regal paraphernalia. Dr de Lusignan has one crown and several medallions in his possession and there are another three Lusignan crowns held in the safe keeping of a Cypriot monastery.

Hard Grind

Now 66 and a former specialist in tuberculosis, he divides his time between Islington, a home in Westcliff-on-Sea and visits abroad, particularly France. He is used to the hard grind of battling against seemingly impossible odds, having spent more than £30,000 in an attempt to establish a claim on estates in Cyprus. On this he still awaits a decision by British, Greek and Turkish interests. He owns other property in England and Turkey.

Next week he will further his claim to the kingdom of Jerusalem by going to the United Nations. 'I'm sure they'll listen to me. After all, they want peace.'

27 June 1967

A HAPPY DOCTOR BLEW BUBBLES

A doctor said at Bow Street Magistrates' Court yesterday that he went to the Eros island at Piccadilly Circus and blew soap bubbles among the crowd because 'bubbles are so pretty and they cheer people up and make them happy'.

Police constables C. Day and G. Ball said some people in the crowd were not amused. Dr Robert Blomfield, aged 29, of Princes Square, Paddington, W, pleaded Not Guilty to insulting behaviour.

With him in the dock was Miss Jane Alexander, aged 26, teacher of art history, also of Princes Square, who denied wilfully obstructing P.C. Ball.

The two officers said Dr Blomfield was told to stop. 'He continued, and when I spoke to him again he turned round and blew a bubble in my face, so he was arrested,' P.C. Day said.

He added that after the arrest Dr Blomfield hung on to railings and began shouting. Miss Alexander intervened and pulled P.C. Ball's arm shouting: 'Get them off him – they're bullies'.

Dr Blomfield said in evidence he had been fairly happy lately and wanted to make others happy. 'Bubbles are a cheap and charming way of doing it,' he said. 'Very few people were annoyed. I did notice a couple of Danes dressed in formal clothing who seemed to think it was childish.'

Mr K. J. P. Barraclough, the Magistrate, said: 'I do not think they were far wrong.'

Miss Alexander in evidence said: 'I was sceptical about it all, but I was really surprised by how cheerful people became when they saw the bubbles.'

Both the accused were given a conditional discharge for six months.

5 August 1967

[Bubble-blowing was also a feature of a 'Flower Folk Love-in' near Slough a few weeks later. The doctor was convicted on 18 August of insulting behaviour whereby a breach of the peace might have been occasioned.]

GIRL'S DEATH IN LEGEND OF CURSE

Miss Evalyn McLean, former joint heiress to the Hope diamond and its reputed curse, was found dead last night at her home in a suburb of Dallas, Texas, where she lived alone. A post mortem examination showed no indication of violence; an analysis of stomach contents is to be made.

Neighbours broke into the house after seeing no activity for several days, and found the body, dressed in blue jeans and sweater, on a bed.

Miss McLean, 25, a former Dallas debutante, quiet-living, was the granddaughter of the late Evalyn Walsh McLean, who said that she paid $40,000 (then £8,000) for the Hope diamond about 60 years ago.

She left it jointly to her six grandchildren when she died in 1947. A dealer bought it from the estate in 1949 and gave it to the Smithsonian Institution in Washington. The grandchildren were never allowed to touch it.

The Hope diamond turned up in London in 1812 and got its name from Henry Thomas Hope, an English banker who bought it in 1830. The story is that the 44½-carat stone was ripped from the forehead of an Indian idol, and came into the hands of a French traveller who was later torn to death by a pack of rabid dogs.

Louis XIV of France is said to have given it to Mme de Montespan as a mark of royal favour, which she lost soon after.

Louis XVI, the legend says, gave it to Marie-Antoinette and it disappeared when they were executed in 1793.

As far as Mrs Evalyn Walsh McLean was concerned, her

first son was killed in a car accident, her husband died in a mental home, and a daughter died of an overdose of sleeping pills in 1946.

The Hope family is said to have fallen on evil days after buying the diamond, and the catalogue of owners in the 16 years before Mrs McLean includes Jacques Colet, who killed himself, Prince Ivan Kanitovitsky, who was murdered, Sultan Abdul Hamid of Turkey, who was dethroned, and a mistress who was murdered: and Simon Montharides, whose carriage was dragged over a cliff by a shying horse killing himself, his wife and their child.

15 December 1967

THE DEVIL'S HOOFMARK – BY A MOUSE?

The exhibition of footprints of famous people in a factory safety campaign hardly breaks new ground: years ago the wild animals and birds of Britain won the distinction of a public display of their footprints, when Mr Alfred Leutscher, the Essex naturalist, wrote a book on the subject, complete with footprint photographs and drawings from nature.

One file in Mr Leutscher's records on animal footprints has now grown bulky – that labelled 'Devil's Hoofmarks'. His explanation that a wood mouse could have caused the mysterious hoofprints in the snow which caused such a sensation in Devon long ago has not gone unchallenged by some observers, though it is generally accepted as a highly likely theory in weightier scientific quarters.

That Devon affair, reported in *The Times* of 16 February 1855, became almost a legend, and still is. Footprints were found at Topsham, Lympstone, Exmouth, and other places which might well have been made by an abominable snow dwarf. They resembled the imprint of a small hoof about 2½ in. across: superstitious people at once saw them as the marks of Satan himself, for sometimes they were even cloven.

The creature seemed to have approached doors and then gone away. Its imprints went up and along walls, over roofs, across high-walled courtyards, and vanished at the foot of

147

walls only to reappear at the other side: clearly the devil could walk straight through a solid wall. People became afraid to go out at night, a local parson spoke reassuringly on the matter from the pulpit, and an armed party sallied out from Dawlish to settle the hash of the mysterious stranger. 'As might be expected, the party returned as they went,' was the dry comment of *The Times* report.

Many Other Theories

Many other theories have been put forward since Mr Leutscher gave his explanation, ranging from a kangaroo to a mooring ring trailing on a rope attached to an escaped balloon. The critic who pointed out that the Devon imprints covered about 100 miles and that this was an impossible feat for one small animal, invited the reply that there was no reason whatever to assume a single animal was responsible, in a county where the wood mouse is abundant.

Mr Leutscher put his theory to the London Zoological Society: he pointed out that an animal when hopping lands with all four feet in a bunch, and in soft snow, especially when it is melting, the result is a U-shaped impression – the 'devil's' footprint. There is only one British animal small enough to have made those Devon tracks – the wood mouse, which can certainly climb and leap. Mr Leutscher has in fact found wood mouse footprints in snow in Epping Forest near his home which exactly conform to the sketches of the Devon imprints.

16 January 1968

THE MAKING OF A PRESIDENT

Governor Reagan's latest and most improbable well-wisher is Mr Joachim Joesten, the irrepressible critic of the Warren Commission. In the appendix to the paperback edition of his latest book, *How Kennedy was Killed*, Joesten publishes the following correspondence between himself and the Governor's office:

Dear Governor Reagan: Why don't you go along with the sensible suggestion to run for Vice-President on a Rockefeller ticket? Then, after selection, all you'd have to do is to invite President Rockefeller to your territory, and ambush and kill him there, say in Los Angeles or San Francisco (the local police might be of some help).

That would make you President – and wouldn't that be nice? With all best wishes for success.
Very truly yours,
Joachim Joesten.

And the Governor's response to this genial advice? 'Dear Mr Joesten,' his secretary is reported to have replied. 'Thank you for taking the time and trouble to write to Governor Reagan and express your interest in the 1968 presidential elections. Governor Reagan appreciates your comments.

'However, the Governor has asked me to reiterate what he has said on many occasions – he is not a candidate for President or for any other national office.'

20 March 1968

GRUESOME CHARADES AT SOTHEBY'S

by Bevis Hillier

Sotheby's had 'some very peculiar telephone calls' after a collection of instruments of torture, sold yesterday, was put on show last week. (One man wanted to know whether they had a branding iron with his initials.) And the showrooms have been the scene of gruesome charades.

On Friday, I saw a male model in parti-coloured tights being genteelly racked in front of whirring cine-cameras. But now these insubstantial pageants have faded, leaving not a rack behind.

The torture instruments extorted £6,752 from impassive bidders yesterday.

The collection of pillories, spiked collars, tongue-tearers, thumbscrews and other grisly apparatus was in the Nuremberg Castle until 1890, when it was bought by Lord Shrewsbury and exhibited extensively in England and America.

Shortly after what Sotheby's catalogue calls, with macabre aptness, the turn of the century, it was acquired by Henry Walters, of Baltimore, Maryland.

Room Packed

In a packed auction room, with cameras clicking and manacles clanking as they were dragged into view by porters, bidding began quite mildly with £30 for 'an unusual viola da gamba-shaped pillory'. But soon the pressure increased, with £48 for a pillory fitted with a weather-vane ('reputedly worn by turncoats and unreliable people'), £50 for iron squatting stocks, and £75 for a tin mask with a *retroussé* and *repoussé* nose, made to the tender specifications of the Holy Inquisition.

A tub-shaped chair, its seat fitted with an iron spike, fetched £90. (For once, Sotheby's did not need to put up polite notices asking buyers kindly to refrain from sitting on the antique furniture.) A whipping bench with a central channel to accommodate the torso made £150 (Naughton) and a rack fitted with a 'spiked hare' roller and a windlass, £350 (J. Bellman).

The most horrifying exhibit was the Iron Maiden, bought for £2,000 by a west German collector, C. Hinckleidey. This fearful instrument, in the form of a madonna-faced girl in early seventeenth-century costume, with hinged doors fixed on the inside with spikes, was used for killing prisoners, who were then dropped into the oblivion of a deep well. Another version of the Maiden, in better condition but probably later in date, was sold in the collection of William Randolph Hearst in 1965 for £2,200.

Use as Propaganda

In 1838, the history of Iron Maidens was traced in 'The Kiss of the Virgin', a scholarly article in *Archaeologia*, the journal of the Society of Antiquaries; later, Bram Stoker, the author of *Dracula*, made one the subject of a blood-curdling story. In 1941, the Maiden was invoked as anti-German propaganda.

26 March 1968

IS HALF UNIVERSE GOING BACKWARDS?

A speculation which implies that half the matter in the universe is going backwards in time is put forward in this week's *Nature* by Dr Kary Mullis, a biochemist at California University.

Dr Mullis's suggestion springs from the union of two physical hypotheses, those of the Schwarzchild singularity and CPT reversal, both of which are on the outermost edge of theoretical knowledge. His theory, briefly, is that when a star or galaxy contracting under its own gravitational force reaches a critical size its component particles undergo a time reversal; travelling in the opposite time direction and composed of anti-matter instead of matter, the galaxy's violent contraction now becomes an equally violent expansion.

20 May 1968

[The 'Schwarzchild singularity', beloved of science-fiction writers, is the critical radius at which a collapsing

151

star begins to exert such a gravitational pull that not even radiation can escape and it becomes a 'black hole'; the remainder of the article – too long to reproduce here – explains the development of the CPT (charge, parity, time) theorem, about the behaviour of subatomic particles, the point being that, in order to maintain symmetry, for every particle with a positive charge, and a directional preference to moving left and going forwards in time, there must be another with a negative charge which prefers to move right and regress into the past. The beauty of Dr Mullis's theory is that it implies a symmetrical universe, in dynamic equilibrium between two states. This would settle the argument as to whether the universe is expanding or contracting: it is doing both to an equal degree and in opposite directions in time.]

MYSTERY OF THE FALLING GEESE

CALGARY, ALBERTA Mr William Holmberg was working on his lawn when geese started falling all around him. He said he heard the honking overhead of a flight of Canada geese and the next minute they started to drop.

Eight of the birds fell over an area of about half a block. One of them crashed through the roof of a house causing damage estimated at about £80. Others fell into gardens and on the street.

Mr Holmberg said: 'The birds were in perfect shape. There does not seem to be any reasonable explanation why they dropped. I thought they had eaten poisoned grain.' Officials from the fish and game branch were equally puzzled. They have sent six of the birds to Edmonton for examination.

4 June 1968

GOLDFISH IS SAVED FROM DROWNING

An RSPCA inspector tonight commended Mr Peter Humphrey, aged 55, for saving a goldfish from drowning, and a full

152

report of the rescue is to be sent to RSPCA headquarters for consideration by the awards committee.

Mr Humphrey discovered the goldfish gasping for air on the surface of his garden pond at Hillside Crescent, Uxbridge, Middlesex. He fished it out and found its mouth was jammed open by a pebble. Gently he went to work and gradually eased the pebble out. Then he put the fish back into the water where it quickly recovered.

Tonight Mr Peter Hume, an RSPCA inspector, said: 'Mr Humphrey's prompt action undoubtedly saved the fish's life. I will be preparing a report to be put before the awards committee.

'There are not many people who know that a fish could drown if it swallows too much water. I would hate to think how many goldfish owners would have stood by and let fish drown because they did not know what was wrong.'

Mr Humphrey, a water purification consultant, said: 'The way the fish was behaving it was obvious to me it was drowning. It kept gasping for air on the surface and then sinking.'

13 August 1968

[Further information on goldfish was adduced in a Science Report later the same year. It was explained that the creature is blessed with exceptionally sharp hearing, enabling it to discriminate between signals as little as one 150 millionth of a second apart.]

NEWTON BARRITT'S SNORING REMEDY

Newton Barritt, who is 80, used to snore so loudly that he woke himself up. But about a year ago, he says, he started to experiment upon himself – he is a retired biochemist – and after two months cured himself. He has since treated six friends in Chester: 'and in every case benign silent sleep was achieved in a period of four to six days'.

Barritt has rejected the common view that snoring is caused by 'posture or mechanical interference with breathing'. His own highly individual theory – which was reached by a combination of intuitive logic and his biochemical training – is that it is due to the effect on the respiratory centre of a failure in the liver's detoxicating function.

And so he arrived at Newton Barritt's Snoring Remedy – which he doesn't wish to bottle himself. He wants to pass it on to the medical world for further investigation: 'I want medical people to take it up. There can't be a monopoly in this.'

Meanwhile here, for afflicted sleepers and their companions, is his concoction: 100 milligrams each of methionine, choline acetate and inositol dissolved in water, to be taken twice a day after meals. A word of warning. It is, he admits, a trifle unpleasant both in taste and smell.

27 September 1968

DIAMOND VEIL FOR MILKY WAY?

Tiny diamond crystals may be an important constituent of the interstellar dust clouds that block our view of vast tracts of the Milky Way. Dr William Saslaw and Dr John Gaustad of the University of California say this would account for features of the clouds that have so far defied explanation.

The manner in which the clouds absorb ultra-violet and infra-red light from distant stars fits in well with the new theory. So does the observation that the material of the clouds can survive the high temperatures existing in parts of the galaxy.

The clouds are so thick in places that they completely hide stars shining beyond them. There is little doubt that the clouds are masses of fine-grained dust particles, but the exact nature of the dust is controversial.

Many astronomers believe that the dust grains are made of carbon in the form of graphite. One view is that the grains are pure graphite, another that they are flakes of graphite coated with a shell of hydrogen ice, feasible in the environment of interstellar space.

Both these suggestions have their drawbacks. Pure graphite does not fit in with the way dust clouds absorb starlight in the far ultra-violet, while ice-coated grains of graphite would be expected to absorb infra-red light more strongly than is observed.

These are two reasons why Dr Saslaw and Dr Gaustad say the dust grains might contain carbon in another form, that of diamond. Diamond and graphite are both composed only of carbon but differ in the way the carbon atoms are arranged among themselves. The dust clouds seem to absorb starlight in much the same way as diamond crystals in the laboratory absorb ultra-violet and infra-red light. Another line of evidence for the new theory may come from the diamonds found in meteorites, until now taken as evidence that meteorites are the remains of the core of exploded planets. But it is disturbing that meteorites do not seem to contain other minerals that ought to have been formed under these conditions.

This is why Dr Saslaw and Dr Gaustad suggest that meteorites may have been formed out of dust clouds, together with the rest of the solar system.

How did diamond come to be in the dust clouds in the first place? There seems to be evidence that carbon atoms in space are more likely to condense in the form of diamond than graphite. The very high temperatures and pressures under which diamonds are found on earth may not be necessary in space.

The two American scientists say that the atmosphere of certain cool stars could be the birthplace of the diamonds. Whether their novel theory will turn out to be correct will depend on detailed measurements of the optical properties of the dust clouds.

10 January 1969

BEETLES AS THIEVES

Seven horned beetles held by the police in Belo Horizonte, Brazil, as accomplices in pilfering, are reported to have died of starvation. The beetles were trained by bus drivers to steal plastic tokens out of the fare boxes, according to the alleged confession of one of 17 drivers accused.

17 February 1969

ANGUISHED HENS

Professor Francois Delaby, a French animal psychiatrist, has produced a novel method of improving the laying productivity of chickens.

Delaby was called in last year by the Farming Society of Villepasson to investigate a decrease in laying locally. He decided that the decrease was caused by 'a phenomenon of anguish' caused by pigeons from a nearby dovecot. In short, the chickens were jealous of the pigeons' flying ability, or, as Delaby expresses it, experienced 'a syndrome of frustrating fixation'.

He recommended artificial altitude treatment for the chickens. They are (as the picture shows) suspended from balloons for up to two hours a day each. Productivity is booming and Delaby is now considering industrial applications of his process.

1 April 1969

[The dangers of this process became apparent when it was reported on 20 August that poachers (presumably balloonists) were fishing for hens by trailing cockroach-baited lines.]

STRANGE ODYSSEY

Among the few possessions found in the pockets of Dr Francesco Saverio d'Ayla, an Italian MP before the Fascists came to power, was his permanent free pass for using the railways, which had enabled him to live largely in trains since the end of the war. He died a few days ago, aged 93.

D'Ayla occasionally found the means to sleep in hotels, but most of his time was spent sitting in trains, reading, talking to other passengers, sleeping, occasionally sharing their snacks with them and then, when the train reached its destination, setting off in another for anywhere. He was always well dressed. He was never without soap, toothbrush and razor. He could talk well in four languages and letters addressed to

'. . . artificial altitude treatment'
[ANGUISHED HENS]

him – sometimes containing small cheques from friends – care of the railway police normally found him within two days at some point in his almost endless odyssey.

Born at Enna in Sicily into a rich family, he entered the diplomatic service and served as 'attaché' in Vienna, London and Paris. When threatened with a posting to northern Europe, he resigned, because he did not like the cold and was in any case not a northern type.

He entered politics, sat in three parliaments as a liberal, but with the rise of fascism chose to live abroad. His election campaigns, exile and devaluation ruined his fortune.

When he returned to Italy after the war, his greatest asset was his permanent railway pass given to members of parliament. His rather severe, solemn appearance became familiar on the trains which for years were his home. He was treated with courtesy by the staffs. When he died he had 1,500 lire in his pocket, exactly £1.

19 May 1969

POLAR BEARS' PICNIC

CHICAGO   Seven escaped polar bears went on a marshmallow rampage at the Brookfield zoo early Thursday morning. When zoo employees arrived for work they were startled to see the bears gathered around a snack bar wolfing down marshmallows and ice cream.

A heavy rainfall had flooded the moat surrounding the bears' enclosure. They swam off their island and made straight for the refreshment stand.

'Apparently they'd been casing that snack bar for more than a year,' a zoo official said.

19 July 1969

PLAN TO KILL HITLER WAS 'UNSPORTING'

A British diplomat suggested a simple way of assassinating

Hitler in 1938 but was told by his Government that it would be 'unsportsmanlike', according to a story in the west German news magazine *Der Spiegel*.

The magazine quoted the draft of an unpublished article and a statement by the daughter of the diplomat, Lieutenant-General Sir Noel Mason MacFarlane, a former Governor of Gibraltar.

General MacFarlane, who died in 1953, was military attaché at the British embassy in Berlin in 1938. He wrote in an unpublished article 17 years ago that he had advocated the assassination of Hitler. All that was needed, he said, was a good gunman and a properly equipped rifle.

Hitler could have been shot from a window during one of his public appearances. The whole plan was worked out in detail, but never written down, according to *Der Spiegel*.

General MacFarlane's daughter, who left her father's papers with the Imperial War Museum, was quoted as saying that Whitehall vetoed the plan. Her father told his family that he had been informed that such a thing would be unsportsmanlike.

Der Spiegel found the draft of the article in the museum. General MacFarlane's conclusion was 'that Hitler's death at that time could have led to the overthrow of National Socialism and that millions of lives could have been saved'. He wrote that Hitler had more than deserved death by the time the assassination was planned.

5 August 1969

[In a leading article the following day the Editor expresses agreement with the above views. Assassinating heads of state, he points out, is illegal. 'No – Britain should not have taken up the General's idea, but should have done something much more substantial in 1938. It should, against the advice of this newspaper, at the time, have stood firm at Munich. That would really have affected history.']

NIXON DELIVERS THE MOON

WASHINGTON President Nixon fulfilled a politician's dream today when he presented governors of the states with pieces of the moon brought back by Apollo II.

'From time immemorial politicians have promised the moon,' the President said. 'I want the record to show that I am the first politician to be able to deliver the moon.'

4 December 1969

UNMISSED ARM

A drunken driver drove on for more than a mile unaware that his right arm had been lopped off by a passing lorry on a road in western Japan. A passer-by found an arm on the highway and notified police. The mystery was solved when a man reported that his right arm was missing.

9 June 1970

RATS PREFER MOZART

Dr Stuart Dimond, a lecturer at University College, Cardiff, told the psychology section about the rat's conservative musical taste when he spoke on investigations of animal behaviour.

The rats were provided with two pedals; one turned on Mozart and the other Schoenberg. The rats took their choice and preferred Mozart.

Their early training brought this result. From infancy they had heard a complete recording of *The Magic Flute*, the fifth violin concerto and two symphonies, all played four times daily.

9 September 1970

FANTASY WORLD OF MAN WHO PLAYED AT SUPERMAN

The bizarre fantasy world of a young man found dead inside a household refrigerator was pieced together yesterday by a Hollywood coroner. Two detectives reported that the man, Mr Arthur Mandelko, aged 24, played at being Superman at night, wearing the appropriate costume. On other occasions he posed as a police officer.

'Every other night', said the dead man's landlord, 'he would climb on the roofs of the bungalows and jump from roof to roof . . . always wearing that Superman outfit.'

He was forced to stop this activity, the landlord said, when other residents complained of the thumping sounds. Instead, Mr Mandelko would combine his two fantasy identities, wearing his Superman outfit under a police uniform. In June police ordered him to stop using a red light and a siren on his motor-cycle.

Three weeks after reporting his tenant missing, the landlord began taking an inventory of the furnished flat. When he opened the refrigerator he found Mr Mandelko's frozen corpse. The dead man was sitting with his knees against his chin. He had been dead, the coroner estimated, for a month. The refrigerator door was held closed from inside by a rope.

The detectives said that in the apartment they found a man-sized robot made of cardboard, rags and tape and a collection of what appeared to be electronic devices, none of which seem to function. They found the Superman suit, a Los Angeles police officer's uniform, a badge and a toy pistol in a wardrobe.

Mr Mandelko was an orphan, the police reported. He had been adopted at the age of 13 and inherited some money when his foster parents died. He left an estate of nearly $45,000 (£18,849).

2 October 1970

UNDERNEATH THE ARCHES

A steady stream of people were climbing the stairs of Nigel Greenwood's Gallery in Glebe Place last week. Irrespective of age, it seemed, or expectations, they became transfixed when they encountered *Singing Sculpture*, by Gilbert and George, who call themselves the 'human sculptors'. These two slight figures, dressed in suits but with their faces painted metallic gold and silver were standing on a table singing the old Bud Flanagan song '*Underneath the Arches*'.

They seemed to be mounted there. They swivelled on their feet with the jerky movements of tiny automats, imitated with great skill. When the tape that they sang to ended, one of them jumped down with a single stiff movement, reset the machine and climbed back. They exchanged the stick and pair of gloves and began again.

The neat, formal monogrammed pamphlets that Gilbert and George always put out with their work are labelled 'art for all'. It is so incongruous that you wonder: is it 'for all', or is it ultra-precious, for a little circle of the art world? Is its oddity to do with the circumstances, a frisson produced by performing a music-hall song in an art gallery? It may be partly these things, and yet it was capable of keeping the attention of a motley footloose audience.

Gilbert and George were sculpture students at St Martin's Art School. They still purposefully call themselves sculptors, although they do not produce objects any longer. In a way their performances have the artificiality of a piece of sculpture. They are contrived in minute detail and perfectly controlled. Gilbert and George don't project anything on the audience or notice them in any way. They seem to exist in a time of their own. Paradoxically, it is this remote self-sufficiency which draws out one's thoughts, to gaze even farther into the distance, beyond their mere actions. Their works are considerable feats of endurance: *Singing Sculpture* was sung continuously for seven hours every day for a week, whether there was anyone present or not. This week they are presenting something different.

17 November 1970

UNION ANGER AT CARTOON STOPS NEWSPAPER

by Chris Dunkley

Production of the London *Evening Standard* was halted yesterday because of a dispute over publication of a cartoon.

Electric plugs to production machinery were pulled out by union members who objected to Jak's cartoon in the first edition of the paper which depicted 'Homo-electrical sapiens Britannicus, *circa* 1970'.

Mr Chataway, Minister of Posts and Telecommunications, said last night: 'This is a direct attack on one of the basic freedoms in any democracy, the freedom of the press.'

The cartoon showed an aggressive cloth-capped individual with his head labelled 'solid bone', eyes 'green with envy', ear 'deaf to reason', mouth 'permanently open', hand 'always out', and a hole where his heart should have been, marked 'nothing here'. In the corner of the cartoon was a framed magnifying glass labelled 'to find brain break glass', and in his hand the man held a newspaper headlined 'Blackout Hits Sick'.

10 December 1970

[The following day a photograph was published of sub-editors of *The Times* working by candlelight.]

VICAR MAKES NUDE ADAM AND EVE FILM

Two girls and a boy are to appear nude in a film directed by the Rev. Cyril Carter, vicar of Hounslow, Middlesex.

Last night Mr Carter said that the film showed the fall of Adam and Eve 'and you can't put Adam and Eve in trousers'.

Eve is played by Miss Helga Lawrence, aged 19, an art student, but she had a phobia about snakes, Mr Carter said, so Gail Atkinson, aged 16, a schoolgirl took the part. Adam is played by Mr John Ruffle, aged 19, a Durham student who lives in the parish.

The film will be shown at Holy Trinity Church in February as part of a youth service.

'We have been very careful with what shots we show and what is out of focus,' Mr Carter said. Parents were asked if they objected.

9 January 1971

[The Rev. Carter later decided to destroy the film, which he had made partly in a private wood and partly in Windsor Safari Park. He said publicity had taken the film out of context.]

WORD SHAPES

A style book has been found like none a working journalist ever consulted. Compiled to inspire the staff of Marsteller (Advertising) and Burton-Marsteller (Public Relations), it is called *The Wonderful World of Words* and launches straight off with the revelation that: 'There are tall, skinny words and short, fat ones, and strong ones and weak ones, and boy words and girl words.'

Examples of lean and lanky words are title, lattice, latitude, lily, and Illinois. Acne is described as a short-fat word – 'even though pimple, with which it is associated, is a puny word'. But there is a difference, we are told, between puny words and feminine words. Feminine words include tissue, slipper, cute, and squeamish; and masculine words include bourbon, rupture and oak: 'Naked is masculine, but nude is feminine.'

Sex isn't always a clear-cut yes or no thing, says the style book. In a fencing team a man may compete with a sabre and that is definitely a masculine word. The book adds: 'Because it is also a sword of sorts, an épée is also a boy word, but you know how it is with épées.'

Words have colours, too. San Francisco is a red city, Cleveland is beige, and Asheville is green. Oklahoma is brown, Florida is yellow, Virginia is light blue and Massachusetts is 'dark green, almost black'. The booklet continues: 'Although they were all Red, at one point Krushchev was red-red, Castro orange, Mao Tse-tung grey, and Kadar black as hate.'

13 April 1971

A COLLECTOR OF FOLLIES AND FANTASIES

by Bevis Hillier

James Reeve, a portrait painter who lives over Olympia Station, is the only modern collector I know who has collected, not to fill elegant cabinets, or to form a series of anything, but simply because these were the things he wanted about him. And what things! There is a wooden baroque shrine with barley-sugar columns. This came from an old colonel in Exeter. Like Reeve, he was a Roman Catholic convert, and when he died his nonconformist housekeeper threw out all the papal trappings. A mummified monkey was given to Reeve by the uncle of Princess Elizabeth of Toro.

On the mantelpiece is a model of Crippen hanging; inside a drawer in the platform is a piece of the rope with which he was hanged. 'Believe it or not, that was given to me as first prize at a children's party when I was six. It was the first object that fired my collection.' Reeve also owns a Victorian trade card printed 'William Marwood. Executioner. 6 Church Lane, Horncastle, Lincolnshire, England.' There are skulls galore, shells, corals, stuffed birds, an eighteenth-century artist's lay figure of boxwood, puppets, advertisements for giants and dwarfs, an egg perched on bird legs, and an ivory snail, emerging with horrible liquescence from its helter-skelter shell. Everywhere there are branches, lianas and great kek stalks: you would think he needed a machete to get to bed.

★ ★ ★

In 1959, Reeve went to Italy. He was invited to a costume party at an American finishing school. 'I wore my death costume – made up by a little *modiste* in Florence, with dead flies stuck all over it. On the way there with my partner, Mary Jo Brant, my motor car gave out, and I had the awful business of pushing it into a garage, dressed as, and feeling like, death. When I was announced at the party, all the servants crossed themselves and fled. I was frightfully hungry. I had hired a skull as an accessory, and during dinner I stuffed it with canapés to take away. When I was introduced to the headmistress, an absolute cornucopia of entrées fell out on the floor.'

In 1963 Reeve went to Spain, and stayed there for five years. On his arrival in Madrid, he went to the circus and met Don Eduardo, the impresario of the dwarfs. He was offered the job of hunting for dwarfs for the circus. 'I travelled the length and breadth of Castile, paying 4,000 pesetas (about £20) for a dwarf. In the minute villages one was received as the Second Coming. Even as late as the nineteenth century, as you probably know, dwarfs were left out on the Sierra to starve or be eaten by wolves.'

Reeve worked for a season at the Circo Pirce, designing costumes and sets for dwarf tableaux. 'My great coup was to discover Doña Alicia, a most beautiful dwarf, whom I painted. She appeared as Marie-Antoinette with a cardboard head which was ceremoniously lopped off with a dinky guillotine. My days with the circus ended abruptly, because of a Peruvian mystic who was in love with me. I introduced her to one of those white-faced sexless clowns with a sequinned hat, and he tried to rape her. I had to leave.'

He rented a studio in the house of the widow of Alfonso XIII's court photographer. 'At one end of the room were all these painted stills of rooms in the palace. Alfonso couldn't take his mistresses to the palace, so he had this brilliant idea of having them photographed against stills of the state rooms. The court photographer had illicitly kept copies of all the photographs. *Paris-Match* would pay a fortune for them. I wish I had got hold of some.'

In Spain he collected things wherever he went. He was given relics by the sacristans of churches. In a monastery outside Segovia he acquired three skulls. 'In repairs to the refectory, several skeletons were found of visiting monks from a sister order, who had been killed by plague in the fifteenth century. The monks wrapped them up for me in greaseproof paper, just like Harrod's, and I took them away in my old jalopy.'

Reeve's main reason for leaving Italy for Spain was to study Velasquez, as an antidote to 'the saccharine horror of Perugino'. Velasquez is still the painter he most admires. He attended the academy – 'the last school in Europe where they still practised the seventeenth century anatomy-school methods of Vesalius. (Since then it has been closed down.) One studied portions of the body. It was valuable to feel the length of a tibia, or to hold an eyeball in one's hand.'

15 May 1971

NUN IN VATICAN HEMLINE CHECK HAS BREAKDOWN

The nun assigned to guard St Peter's Basilica from immodestly dressed tourists was withdrawn today from her post after suffering a nervous breakdown. She said she could no longer stand the taunts from tourists, the shoving from photographers and the jibes in the press.

During the past few weeks Sister Fiorella (Little Flower) had refused entry to thousands of women in miniskirts, see-through blouses, low-cut sweaters and skirt and trousers combinations which left midriffs bare.

Sister Fiorella was the first woman assigned to security work by the Vatican. Vatican sources said it was thought a woman was less likely than a man to give in to a pretty girl's arguments and angry tourists were less likely to cause a disturbance if dealing with a nun.

5 August 1971

[According to a report the following August the problem was eventually solved by lending 'long, rather lugubrious garments in black plastic' to visitors considered insufficiently clad.]

CATFISH TO BE KILLED AT ART EXHIBITION

by Peter Hopkirk

Sixty live catfish will be publicly electrocuted by an American artist at the Hayward Gallery tomorrow in a bizarre art exhibition.

Flown from the United States at the invitation and expense of the Arts Council, together with 22 lobsters, 100 oysters and thousands of shrimps, the catfish will be displayed for the next six weeks in six huge tanks at the gallery. They form one of the 11 items in an exhibition there of Los Angeles modern art.

Called 'Portable Fish Farm', the tanks forming the exhibit are made of plywood and glass fibre and are lined with rubber.

Three of the 20-ft-long tanks contain a total of 300 catfish, eight of which weigh 4 lb each.

Tomorrow, between 9 and 10 a.m., the artist, Mr Newton Harrison, aged 39, will 'harvest' 60 of the medium-size catfish, each weighing about 2 lb. After removing each with a net he will kill it by placing it in a 'death chamber' through which an electrical charge will be passed.

The fish will next be prepared by Mr Harrison for a 'celebration feast', which is due to take place in the evening and which is organized by the Contemporary Arts Society.

Later in the exhibition lobsters, oysters and shrimps will suffer the same ritualistic fate. The Arts Council hopes that members of the public, who pay a 40p entrance charge for the exhibition, will take part in the feasts after the killings.

An Arts Council official described the exhibit last night as 'intensely original and exciting'. He said he hoped people would take it seriously.

Mr Harrison told me that killing the fish by electrocution was the most humane way that could be devised. 'It takes only about two seconds to kill each fish,' he said.

He said those who were critical should realize that films using horses and fishermen using hooks were far more cruel.

29 September 1971

[The RSPCA protested at the proposed electrocution. So

did the comedian Spike Milligan, whose protest took the form of smashing a window of the Hayward Gallery, for which he afterwards paid. Meanwhile, Hugh Willat, Secretary General of the Arts Council, after consultation with the chairman, Lord Goodman, decided that it would be wrong to kill the catfish and the electrocution was called off.]

BABY ABANDONED IN MANGER

HOUSTON   Two women stood admiring the nativity scene at St Anne's Roman Catholic Church. Suddenly the baby in the manger began to move.

The abandoned baby boy, less than 1 month old, has been placed in a foster home by the county welfare department.

1 January 1972

MOON SHOTS, THE CAMBODIAN WAY

PHNOM PENH   Two people were killed and nearly 50 injured by spent bullets when hundreds of Cambodian troops opened fire at the moon.

The soldiers fired into the sky to prevent an eclipse of the moon by a mythical monster frog, called Reahou. According to ancient Cambodian legend the giant frog wants to eat the moon and must be stopped.

1 February 1972

ELEPHANT LOST ITS INTEREST IN SKIING

LOS ANGELES   Bimbo, the elephant who lost interest in dancing and water skiing after being injured in a road accident, has won accident damages in a court case here. Judge Julius Title of the California Supreme Court ruled that the driver of a car which collided with Bimbo's trailer three years

'. . . wants to eat the moon'
[MOON SHOTS, THE CAMBODIAN WAY]

ago should pay $4,500 (£1,750) damages to the elephant's owner.

26 February 1972

MUSSOLINI'S PASSPORT SOLD FOR £1,200

by Geraldine Norman

Mussolini's passport in a gilt-morocco case stamped with the crest and motto of Ian Fleming, of James Bond fame, is a collectors' item with a remarkable dual association. It commanded £1,200 at Sotheby's yesterday. The passport itself dates from 1922, the year of the famous march on Rome which brought Mussolini to power.

When the Milan police issued this seedy brown regulation passport, Mussolini was still a 'journalist'. The only two journeys he made with it were to France in January and Germany in March as editor of the *Popolo d'Italia*. On the first he interviewed the French Prime Minister, Briand, in Cannes and on the second the German Chancellor, Wirth, in Berlin.

In addition to Ian Fleming, the passport has belonged to A. J. A. Symons, author of *The Quest for Corvo*. It was given to him by Maundy Gregory, a mysterious and celebrated figure, who acquired it about 1930, although how and where is unknown.

10 May 1972

ONASSIS PLATE-SMASHING 'BROKE THE LAW'

An Athens lawyer asked the public prosecutor today to take penal action against Mr Aristotle Onassis, the shipowner, and his son, for violating the regime's ban on smashing plates in public.

Plate-smashing, once a favourite pastime of Greek revellers, was banned by decree on 31 December 1968. It was condemned as a barbarian practice offending 'the noble traditions and mores of Greek society'. The custom, which had gained great popularity with foreign tourists here, became an offence punishable by up to six months' imprisonment.

Two days ago the Athens press published photographs of Mr Onassis and his son, Alexander, entertaining a galaxy of international film stars at an Athens nightclub. Stacks of plates were in evidence on their table and so was the smashed crockery on the dance floor. The headline ran: 'Olympic plate-smashing record goes to Onassis'.

Mr Nikolaos Galeadis, a barrister, informed the press tonight that he had petitioned the prosecutor to institute penal proceedings against Mr Onassis and his son.

The petition described the plate-smashing scene as a 'bacchic orgy' and a 'ritual'. It pointed out that, on the same day, the same newspapers had reported the news of the arrest of a 25-year-old painter for smashing plates during a night-out in the country.

Two or three Greeks have been tried and convicted since the ban was imposed, but, giving in to pressure from tourist establishments, the authorities seem to be turning a blind eye. But Mr Galeadis said that one of his clients had been made to serve 15 days in jail for smashing one plate in a *taverna*.

In his petition, Mr Galeadis quoted a recent statement by Mr Pattakos, the First Deputy Prime Minister, urging equality in the application of the law to avoid giving the impression that Isocrates had been right in saying: 'The law is like a spider's web. It catches the insects, but lets the bigger animals through to escape.'

14 September 1972

MONNA LISA SMILE GROWS MORE PUZZLING

by Tim Jones

The Monna Lisa's smile threatens to break into a grin in the light of claims yesterday that the original lady hangs in the red drawing room in the home of Lord Brownlow, one of Britain's richest peers, or in a Kensington flat.

Lord Brownlow, a lifelong friend of the late Duke of Windsor, said: 'It would be wrong of me to debunk that masterpiece that hangs in the Louvre and say mine is the original. All I say is that the La Gioconda that hangs on my wall was painted on wood by da Vinci.'

The claim may bring a challenge from the heavily fortified Kensington flat of Dr Henry Pulitzer, an art dealer. He believes that the original lady nestles between the electronic protective devices at his home.

Lord Brownlow becomes particularly upset when he recalls how the French wanted to borrow his painting for an exhibition in Paris. 'The request came in a letter and I saw no harm in letting them have it, provided they made all the insurance arrangements,' he said. 'I was actually penning a letter telling them of this when I noticed in the margin of their letter that the exhibition was being staged by the French "Scotland Yard" and was to be entitled "The World's Greatest Forgeries".

'My painting is not a forgery and I certainly was not going to allow it to be hung alongside dud banknotes and the like. Like all painters of that time da Vinci did not just paint one of a subject.'

News of Lord Brownlow's Monna Lisa became known when he heard that the Louvre had refused to lend its painting for a celebration exhibition in London and offered his instead.

This could be embarrassing because Dr Pulitzer has indicated that if he is approached he may consider allowing his Monna Lisa to be shown at the same exhibition.

Dr Pulitzer, who was born in Vienna, says he sold his home and its contents in 1962 to buy his painting. Since then, the former gentleman-in-waiting to King Zog of Albania has spent much time gathering information to prove that his purchase is authentic. According to him, Leonardo painted two versions of the Monna Lisa.

Lord Brownlow recalls that in his boyhood the Leonardo stood on an easel at his family's other home in the south of England. 'Every night two footmen would come into the room and with great ceremony carry the painting away to a strong room where it was locked up for the night.

'The painting came into my family after the death of Sir

Joshua Reynolds, who, I understand, prized it most highly.'

Shadowing under the eyes was done in ink, not paint like the one in the Louvre, he said. Leonardo apparently often favoured ink for shadowing.

Only one person, it seems, knows for certain which painting is the original. And she is not saying.

Last night an art expert said: 'It is possible but not very probable that more than one Monna Lisa was painted by da Vinci. All known records refer to only one such work.'

17 October 1972

[Correspondents were intrigued by the spelling of 'Monna' with two 'n's. One of them congratulated the author on his article, while others suggested that the three Giocondas were respectively the Mona, the Monna and the Monnna . . . the beauty of this explanation being that it could be extended to the *nth* degree.]

CRAVING FOR LIQUORICE

A craving for liquorice may be a diagnostic sign of Addison's disease, according to Dr J. A. Cotterill and Dr W. J. Cunliffe of Leeds General Infirmary.

The disease, a consequence of defective functioning of the adrenal glands, is characterized by fatigue, depression, loss of weight and an unusual skin colour. The usual treatment involves daily injections of cortisone, but in some cases the symptoms can be relieved by taking liquorice extract.

Dr Cotterill reports the case of a woman who had had all the symptoms of Addison's disease for two or more years, during which time she had been eating about 12 oz of Pontefract cakes daily. Dr Cotterill and Dr Cunliffe calculate that that would amount to a daily dose of between 10 and 12 grams of liquorice extract. The patient insisted that the Pontefract cakes had alleviated the feeling of tiredness and generally made her feel better.

About six weeks before she complained to her doctor, however, the self-treatment with Pontefract cakes had ceased to be effective. Dr Cotterill and Dr Cunliffe suggest that that may have been because the disease had progressed beyond the point at which liquorice is an effective treatment: it seems to work only when the adrenal glands are still partly functional. They treated her with the usual cortisone therapy and a day after treatment was begun the craving for liquorice disappeared.

Self-medication with liquorice seems to have been reported in only a few other cases of Addison's disease, but Dr Cotterill and Dr Cunliffe believe it may be fairly common and therefore a potentially useful diagnostic tool. It is well known that patients often develop a craving for salt, which also tends to restore the imbalance caused by Addison's disease.

It may be unwise in general to dismiss strange cravings as of psychological rather than physiological significance. For example, pregnant women are frequently accused of outrageously irrational food preferences, which on careful analysis can probably be often attributed to attempts to correct iron deficiency.

14 February 1973

CARDBOARD POLICE FORCE PROPOSED

Motorists driving through Alrewas, Staffordshire, on the A38, will notice a marked rise in the number of policemen watching their progress if a village plan is approved. But the officers will be made of cardboard.

Parish councillors, who have pressed unsuccessfully for a speed limit on the dual carriageway through the village, are considering a proposal to use life-size models of policemen.

25 April 1973

MOSQUITO BEATS WHITE MAN

FREETOWN   The malaria-carrying mosquito was honoured in Sierra Leone today for making the country the 'white man's grave' in the past and preventing Europeans settling here.

The Order of the Mosquito has been created to reward acts of military or civil gallantry, the President's office announces.

8 May 1973

REAR VIEW

The triennial prize at Oxford University for an English poem on a sacred subject has as its text for 1974: 'Thou shalt see my back parts; but my face shall not be seen' (Exodus 33:23). Competitors, who must have qualified for a university degree, have to write not fewer than 60 and not more than 300 lines of decasyllabic verse on this hindsighted theme, rhymed in couplets, stanzas, or as blank verse. They are not allowed to resort to dramatic form.

The subject was chosen by the judges who awarded the last prize to Rachel Trickett, now principal-elect of St Hugh's College. They included the present professor of poetry, Roy Fuller, but he says: 'The idea for next year's subject was not mine. I wish I could claim the credit for it – it seems to open up a number of intriguing possibilities.'

13 July 1973

IF MUSIC BE THE FOOD OF LOVE

TUNIS   President Bourguiba, in an appeal for better family planning in Tunisia, told a meeting here that one man in Ksar Hellal had been able to form a full orchestra from his forty children.

'He is the father of forty children born to him by four wives, with whom he has created a complete orchestra,' he said. 'This is something which is utterly scandalous.'

22 September 1973

FRENCHMAN KILLS SECOND WIFE FOR BAD COOKING

PARIS   A man was today sent to prison for eight years for killing his second wife – as he did his first – because her cooking was not up to cordon bleu standard. The judge told Noël Carriou, aged 54, in passing sentence, that he understood good cooking was an important part of married life.

The court was told that M. Carriou killed his second wife after she cooked him an overdone roast. Seventeen years ago, enraged because he had been served with undercooked meat, he threw his first wife out of bed so violently that she broke her neck.

After seven years in prison he was released for good conduct and soon married again. Then one Sunday, already infuriated by a religious programme on television, M. Carriou quarrelled with his wife over an overcooked roast.

The jury found that he did not intend to murder his wife and recommended leniency.

17 November 1973

MPs PROTEST AT 'ROMANCE IN THE BATH'

MPs are protesting about a Gas Board advertisement urging couples to share a bath to save fuel. The South Eastern Gas Board (Segas) advertisement shows a couple sharing a bath, with this comment: 'Put a bit of romance into your bath by sharing the water.'

Mr John Stokes, Conservative MP for Oldbury and Halesowen, said: 'It is deplorably vulgar and in the worst possible taste. There is not much one can do about it, but I find it extraordinary coming from a nationalized industry from whom we ought to be able to expect the highest standards.'

Another protest came from Mr Joseph Kinsey, Conservative MP for Birmingham, Perry Barr, who commented: 'I am shocked. It is debasing the standards of the Gas Board to suggest that we should share our baths.'

The bath-time hint came from a 'Mrs Jones of East

Molesey', Surrey, and she won £10 for it in a Segas competition.

28 January 1974

[The following day *The Times* reported an interview with Mrs Ida Jones, who remarked 'I cannot understand what all the fuss is about.' Neighbours supported her. One of them said 'People have been sharing a bath for years. There is nothing wrong in it. It is better than having a rubber duck.']

'LOST WORLD' UNCHANGED IN MILLIONS OF YEARS

CARACAS A British explorer who descended into an untrodden crater in the Venezuelan jungle said here today it contained millions of nuts piled up over centuries by migrant birds.

The nuts were among a number of unusual finds described by Mr David Nott, aged 45, a British mountaineer and one of three men who returned here yesterday after six days in the 800-ft-deep pit.

The nuts had been piled up by guacharos which lived in a crack in the crater, Mr Nott said.

Mr Nott, a former instructor at the Eskdale Outward Bound school, went into the unexplored crater near the Brazilian frontier with Dr Charles Brewer Carias, the expedition leader and an official of the Venezuelan Natural Science Society, and his brother Jimmy.

Mr Nott said they had brought back carnivorous plants, small insects, shrubs and other living organisms apparently unique. The crater's interior was older than the Andes he said, and had soil, humidity and acidity characteristics which obtained on the rest of the Earth millions of years ago.

The only discomfort in the 'lost world' was the lack of fresh air in the crater, which made breathing difficult and movement heavy, although the ground on the bottom was very dry even in places where the jungle was inpenetrable, Mr Nott said.

The explorers' support teams were understood to be continuing preparations for a descent into a second, smaller crater and an exploration of two nearby plateaux.

One support group returned to Caracas to fetch a special ladder to avoid the difficulties the team had climbing out of the first crater, which led to earlier reports that they were trapped.

20 February 1974

FRUITFUL

God and Mammon have rarely been as closely linked as in the literature sent out by the Rev. T. L. Osborn. Osborn, who appears to be based in America, says he has 'found the secret that unlocks God's great storehouse of plenty'. This handily discovered key is his Pact of Plenty, 'the Soulwinning Pact that is prospering thousands financially'.

It is a sort of pay as you pray scheme. The chosen are sent the Pact of Plenty pamphlet, which has 12 identical slips ordering them to 'Honour the Lord with thy first fruits'. First fruits are £2 a month per prayer, and for the true believer (or the truly credulous) an invitation to send more.

Free with all this comes Osborn's advice on how to manage the pact with God. 'Even if you must do without something you need for a while, put your prayer money of £2 inside the postpaid envelope with your Prayer slip . . . Around the 1st, when mission needs are most urgent, plant those first fruits in this ministry, then watch for miracles as God returns his plenty to you.'

Given sufficient faith and the £2 a month down payment on it, Osborn promises a steady stream of miracles. 'People get better jobs, salary increases, new homes and cars, inheritances, business benefits.' All you have to do is 'do it the Jesus Way and Prosper'.

I wanted to ask him how his little sideline in miracles was coming along, and telegrammed his Birmingham box number. But neither he nor a representative of his Osborn Founda-

179

tion has yet taken this opportunity to spread the word further through the press.

26 June 1974

THE MYSTERY OF EQUATORIAL BATHS

NAIROBI   A Kenyan cameraman has answered a call by Yorkshire Television to film water flowing out of a bath at the Equator.

The company wanted to test a theory that, because of the earth's rotation, water flows clockwise out of plugholes in the southern hemisphere, anti-clockwise in the northern hemisphere and straight down at the Equator. 'The water went straight down,' reported the cameraman.

13 July 1974

NAMES

The vicar of St Philip and St James's, Oxford, the Reverend A. Saint, has written to say that he was once introduced by a parishioner as 'our new vicar, Mr Satan'. Until a few years ago, his churchwarden was Mrs A. Martyr. While we are on the subject, the secretary of the National Association of Funeral Directors has the encouraging name, Ray Heaven.

23 August 1974

MORE NAMES

The head of the dogs section of Merseyside Police is Inspector Barker, and the secretary to the department of medieval history at University College, Dublin, is Mrs Serff. At the end of the last war, the bursar of Magdalen College, Oxford, was named Cook, the cook was named Butler and the butler was named Chamberlain.

11 September 1974

DUKE FOUND IN CAR PARK WAITING FOR END OF WORLD

GENEVA   An Italian duke and duchess, missing since June, have been found living penniless with a bizarre sect in the car park of Geneva airport.

When found, a woman member of the sect had been dead for five days from a lung infection. The police said the sect had been expecting the end of the world last weekend.

Duke Melzi Deril and his wife set out from the Bergamo area in June with an unfrocked parish priest, who leads the sect, and 15 others.

The group travelled all over Europe, staying at the best hotels on the duke's money until funds ran out, the police said. Without money and hungry, they washed and drank water in the airport toilets.

17 October 1974

WHAT BANGKOK IS FAMOUS FOR

[The *Times* Diarist samples the delights of a Bangkok massage parlour.]

We sat on the stone bench and waited for the beer to arrive. Conversation was difficult since Number 249 had about a dozen words of English and I no Thai. 'American?' she hazarded. 'English,' I replied. 'I no English,' she said, concluding the conversation.

The beer came, with a cola for 249. I did not have the right change (20 *baht*) so there was a further long delay while we waited for change to be brought. I sipped a mouthful and 249 pointed to the beer and inquired: 'Number One?' 'Number One,' I agreed.

Meanwhile she had run a bath which was standing, getting cool. By the time the financial transactions were completed and she motioned me to climb in, it was no more than lukewarm. I have had hotter baths for less at Porchester Hall in Bayswater, but there you do not get the same attention.

Number 249 washed me thoroughly. There was only one untoward incident, an undignified scramble when she dropped the soap, rather out of keeping with the sense of repose the surroundings were supposed to encourage.

She let the water out and aimed the shower at my head and torso, soaping me some more. Some soap painfully entered my left eye, and 249 laughed.

Next came a bubble bath, with the bubbles rubbed pleasantly into my skin. A shower completed the wet section.

By that time, taking into account the early delays over the beer order, there was precious little time left for formal massage. I climbed on the couch, which was the signal for 249 to try, in sign language, to sell me an extra hour, with a promise of untold delights. I resisted. 'You must understand that I work for *The Times*,' I said, by way of explanation.

Then she made further suggestions which I assume were only in fun. 'You Number One,' she said. 'You Number 249,' I quipped, but she did not see the joke.

22 November 1974

BORING

In any competition to discover the most boring institution in the country, accountants would win by acclamation, if that is not too vigorous a word for it. They would be followed by the TUC and the EEC Commission.

But the leaden supremacy of these in the tedium stakes was subjected to a prolix and wooden challenge in Leeds yesterday. A dozen academics at the university set out to underwhelm each other and a panel of student judges with a four-minute performance at the lectern. They sought to carry off the Golden Pillow Award for the most boring lecturer in the world.

Contributions included an eminently forgettable disquisition on the Scunthorpe School of Ethno-Methodology delivered in an Alan Bennett vicar voice by Dr Huga Meynall, a theological philosopher.

Victory, and the Golden Pillow stuffed with shredded

lectures, went inevitably to an applied scientist. Dr Ashley Clarke is one of nature's heavies and, in the old phrase, the sort of bore who is here today and here tomorrow.

He delivered boredom by the megaton with an account of Mechanical Formalism of Emulsion in an Infinite Viscous Medium. 'I was going to call it the classic hydraulic formalism of emulsion in an infinite viscous medium but I didn't want to excite you all,' he droned.

After scratching a mass of indecipherable formulae on a blackboard, Dr Clarke ended painfully and pointlessly with: 'This only applies in an *infinite* viscous medium, so in practice it doesn't work.'

3 December 1974

PANDA SCREAMED A WARNING OF EARTHQUAKE

PEKING   Children in the city of Tientsin have been advised to watch the behaviour of animals in the zoo as a means of predicting earthquakes.

The panda held its head and screamed in 1969 when there was an earthquake in the Gulf of Pohai, it was stated in a broadcast for children on Tientsin Radio. Turtles became agitated, and the tiger, the swan and the yak lay down on the ground when they felt the tremors.

The broadcast also said that well water could rise or sink or change its composition as a sign that an earthquake was in the offing. There were preliminary tremors before a big upheaval, and visible electric discharges were given off by the ground.

There was no direct reference to the recent earthquake in Manchuria but it is known the authorities believe there may soon be another one in the Tientsin area, which is about 75 miles from Peking.

20 February 1975

HOSTEL PLAN FOR THE DEPRAVED

A hostel in London for the treatment of 'victims of moral pollution' is being planned by the Festival of Light. Pornography addicts, sexual deviants and 'others involved in erotica' would follow a course of compulsory spiritual activities and handicrafts.

An appeal is being considered for the project, which would cost about £3,000 an inmate. Residents, at first only males will be considered, would contribute sick benefit or social security payments to help to meet running costs.

2 May 1975

JUMP SAVES LIFT CRASH MAN

A man in a falling lift escaped almost unhurt yesterday by

jumping into the air a moment before impact. Four men with him were seriously injured.

Mr James Shearer, aged 27, a glazier, was in an industrial lift which fell 60 ft at a Liverpool building site. He suffered slight ankle injuries.

9 May 1975

POLICE MOVE ON WIDOWS WHO COHABIT

from Peter Evans

A medieval ceremony for contrite widows was quoted at the Police Federation's annual conference in Blackpool yesterday in support of a move to ensure that widows of policemen do not lose their pensions if they cohabit.

Under one section of the police pension regulations a policeman's widow may lose her pension if she lives with another man, but can apply to get it back if she has given up the association.

Chief Inspector David Howell, of Wiltshire, told delegates that in medieval times when the widow of a land holder formed a sexual relationship with a man her lands could be taken away from her.

In some parts of the country, however, there was provision for the lands to be returned to her if she went through a ritual.

It consisted of her going into the next court held in the manor, riding backwards on a black ram with the tail in her hand, saying:

> Here I am, riding upon a black ram,
> just like the whore I am.
> And for my crinkum crankum,
> have lost my binkum bankum.
> And for my tail's game,
> am brought to this worldly shame.
> Therefore, good master steward,
> let me have my lands again.

Mr Howell said to the best of his knowledge Wiltshire police authority did not insist upon the black ram but the principle was the same: that of public humiliation.

The conference passed a resolution calling for the regulation to be abolished.

30 May 1975

AN INSIDIOUS AND CORROSIVE MENACE

Dr Athol Gallifent of Kensington has found a grave omission from the report on *Dogs in the United Kingdom* published earlier this month by the dog-loving Joint Advisory Committee on Pets in Society. There was a brief mention of fouling ('stray dogs are known to foul in public places' it said mildly of the four tons of dog excrement which are deposited in London alone each day) but not a word about the dogs' success in causing the collapse of lamp standards by urinating against them.

Gallifent claims that he saw one modern steel lamp standard crash down in a central London street this month, and that he knows of several more which are 'distinctly wobbly'. Elegant standards painted in old gold (the sort which line several prestige shopping areas) are, he warns, particularly vulnerable.

The local authorities charged with the maintenance of London's lamp standards confirm Gallifent's charges. This hitherto undiscussed urban menace is, they say, a familiar and continuing problem. It is calculated that 3,000 pints of canine urine are released in London each day.

The deputy borough engineer of Lambeth said: 'We undertook quite a lot of research into this problem in our borough about 15 years ago. We found that dog urine is particularly corrosive.

'We tried galvanizing the bases, using thicker standards, switching to cast iron and more recently protecting many street signposts with grey plastic sleeves. Corrosion does still take place, and some of our standards had to be taken down because they had become unstable and dangerous. It is now general policy in the borough to switch from steel to concrete, which is not affected as long as the surface does not get cracks in it.'

A foreman in charge of a street lighting maintenance team in south London said: 'Anybody can see the damage the dogs do. Look on the larger columns about two feet up from the ground and you will see a band which the dogs have obviously fouled frequently and persistently. The deterioration in the paint work and the metal sets in very quickly, and when you have to go to work on it, believe me it smells dreadful too.'

In Westminster, the city council have tried to protect standards with galvanized skirts, blast-spraying with zinc and fresh coats of paint every three years, but they admit they still have a problem. 'The steel standards which were in the old borough of Marylebone and which we inherited at the amalgamation', said a section superintendent, 'have always been a

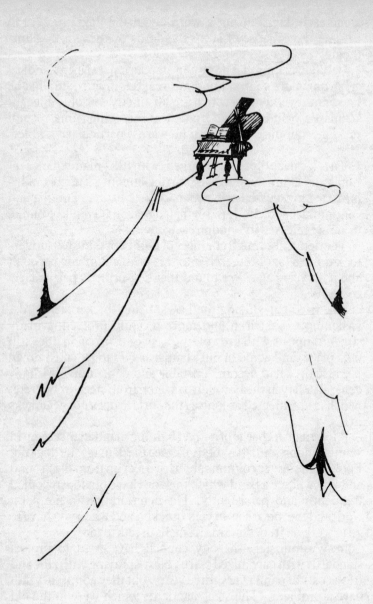

'. . . up a 6,500 ft peak'
[MUSIC REACHES HIGHEST NOTE]

problem, and we are in course of replacing them because they have become a danger.

'Dog urine has certainly been a contributory factor. No doubt there are local authorities still buying plain steel standards, but perhaps they are in areas where they don't have dog problems on our sort of scale.'

28 July 1975

[A few days later it was reported that during the war airmen were circularised with a daily order headed 'Corrosion of magnesium alloy aircraft landing wheels – promiscuous urination.' Analysis had shown a high percentage of urea in damaged wheels. Later the airmen were exonerated, however, since the authorities came to the conclusion that the culprits were dogs straying onto relief landing grounds.]

MUSIC REACHES HIGHEST NOTE

INNSBRUCK Eighteen muscular mountaineers today claimed a new feat for the record books – hauling a grand piano up a 6,500-ft peak in the Austrian Alps.

The piano will stay on the Gschollkopf peak in the Tyrol until the skiing season starts. It took three hours to get the instrument to the summit on Friday.

8 September 1975

ALL SYSTEMS GO-GO ON NUCLEAR SUBMARINE

Because he permitted a young woman to dance topless on the deck of the American nuclear attack submarine *Finback* as it left port last July, its captain has been relieved of his command, pending an investigation.

Commander Connally Stevenson, aged 41, explained to interviewers today that his acquiescence in a 'consensus request from officers and men' was intended as a reward for all

189

the hard work they had done in completing the ship's overhaul ahead of schedule.

The crew had appreciated the talents of Miss Cat Futch, age 23, at a night club near Port Canaveral, Florida, and the idea was to score off the crew of the *Alexander Hamilton*, a missile-firing ship tied up close by.

Apparently the *Hamilton*'s crew gaped in admiration as the *Finback* left port with go-go music playing and Cat Futch doing her cavorting before the assembled crew.

That was 10 July, and no one sneaked at first. Then on 1 August the Navy command suddenly radioed the submerged vessel in mid-Atlantic to return to port. Commander Stevenson is undergoing a 'captain's mast' – a non-judicial review.

The shapely Miss Futch, who disembarked with the pilot as the submarine left port, said she could not believe the United States Navy could be so severe. 'I know quite a bit about the Navy', she exclaimed, 'and I never saw such a smiling bunch of men go out to sea. It really boosted the men's morale.'

10 September 1975

MIRABILIS

An admirer of the Conservative Party leader has drawn my attention to *The Hamlyn Guide to Shells of the World*, which contains a full description and illustration of *Thatcheria mirabilis*. 'One of the most fascinating of all shells', it says. 'About eight whorls with very angular shoulders and small carina . . .

'Body narrows sharply to wide, open siphonal canal. Wide aperture; simple, thin lip; and slightly concave and extended columella. Smooth but with very fine, spiral threads and weak growth lines. Pinky tan to tan; interior white.' No true blue anywhere, so it cannot be the same person.

6 October 1975

FOSSILIZED

Still more news about *Thatcheria mirabilis*, the seashell with political affiliations. This time my authoritative source is Dr John Taylor of the Mollusca Section of the British Museum (Natural History).

The shell, he writes, is 'the last surviving species of a family prolific in the geological past but now, alas, found only as fossils. It tends to be found in rather deep water . . . Although it has a rather beautiful exterior appearance, its mouth is equipped with dart-like teeth which, combined with a venomous salivary secretion, immobolize the prey (mainly worms).'

The shell was named in 1877 after a Charles Thatcher, who brought it back from Japan. One G. W. Tryon said of it: 'That this shell is a scalariform monstrosity cannot be doubted, but what may be its natural form is not so readily ascertained.'

9 October 1975

MORTALITY: FLORAL BURIAL

The custom of placing flowers on the graves of the dead goes back to the very beginnings of civilization and can provide archaeologists with a means of bringing the past vividly to life. Modern techniques of pollen analysis have now shown that one day in early summer, more than 50,000 years ago, a Neanderthal man discovered by archaeologists 15 years ago in the Zagros mountains of Iraq, and named Shanidar IV, was laid in his grave on a bed of brilliantly coloured wild flowers.

Arlette Leroi-Gourham of the Musée de l'Homme in Paris has analysed the pollen found in the Shanidar IV grave and describes in a recent issue of *Science* how the grave may have been arranged. Large clusters of pollen of various types of flowers were found, in the soil under the skeleton, some still in the form of the anther, showing that the pollen had not simply blown in from the outside.

The most abundant pollen came from flowers of the *Senecio* family – the ragworts which have bright golden yellow flowers, and from *Achillea*, which contains yellow and creamy

191

white flower species. Pollen from the yellow St Barnaby's thistle was also identified, as well as several clusters of the brilliant blue *Muscari*, wild relatives of the garden grape hyacinth. Mixed in with them were clusters of pollen from *Ephedra*, whose flexible, highly branched stems lend themselves well to the construction of bedding on which the dead could have been laid.

In one of the samples a scale from a butterfly's wing was found among the pollen and, as the author remarks, it needs little imagination to suppose that a butterfly had alighted on one of the flowers and was later brought into the cave.

Nowadays, in the Zagros mountains, the flowers found in the cave bloom during May and June, so, even allowing for a slight shift in the flowering period as a result of a change in the climate from the more humid conditions then obtaining, Shanidar IV was undoubtedly laid in his grave sometime between the end of May and early July.

12 November 1975

ADELAIDE PREPARES TO MEET ITS DOOM

On the eve of its predicted 'doomsday', this South Australian city is awaiting the appointed hour with lively interest, but is refusing to quake with fear.

Private homes are rocking to 'pre-earthquake parties', massage parlours are offering 'tidal wave specials' and car dealers are advertising 'crumbling prices'. But Mr John Nash, the clairvoyant house painter, who said the city of 800,000 people would be destroyed at about noon tomorrow by an earthquake and a tidal wave, was nowhere to be found. He was last heard of in Melbourne, 400 miles away.

Despite the mood of disbelief, Mr Richard Sterling, a prominent Australian astrologer, said on Friday that planetary influences supported Mr Nash's prophecy of doom. He predicted that South Australia would be hit by disaster either tomorrow or on Tuesday.

Some immigrants in Adelaide have left the city for the hills after hearing rumours of disaster. A community leader said that because of language difficulties the immigrants were 'not aware of the scientific evidence published over the past few days refuting the prediction'.

One man who is out to prove there is nothing in it at all is Mr Don Dunstan, the South Australian Premier. He has promised to stand Canute-like on Gleneig beach tomorrow.

A jetty near by will be the venue for an 'earthquake party'. Guests have been asked to wear flippers, a snorkel and bow tie and the host has promised to leave plastic bottles in which the partygoers can leave distress messages.

19 January 1976

[Needless precautions indeed, for, in the words of *The Times* report the following day 'Doomsday slipped by Adelaide without a ripple'.]

ROMSEY ABBEY WORKMEN DISCOVER ROSE WITH PETALS INTACT AFTER 850 YEARS

by Philip Howard

Workmen have discovered what seems to be the oldest botanical specimen ever found in Europe in the east wall of Romsey Abbey. It is a rose, hidden in the wall more than eight and a half centuries ago.

The oldest rose in the world was discovered romantically two days before St Valentine's day, by workmen removing medieval paintings from the east wall. They noticed that the putlog holes, used by workmen in the Middle Ages to support scaffolding, had been uncharacteristically plastered over.

They removed the plaster and found the rose, about an inch and a half in diameter, with a twig and numerous petals and leaves. It is wizened and sere, very fragile, but perfectly preserved.

Yesterday Dr Jane Renfrew, a paleobotanist, spent four hours removing it with infinitesimal delicacy, and it was taken to London for conservation treatment at the Natural History Museum.

Mr Kevin Stubbs, director of archaeology for the Test Valley, says that the rose can be dated precisely. The *terminus ante quem* is 1270, when the wall paintings were made over the undisturbed putlog holes.

Mr Stubbs says: 'However, there was no reason for the putlog holes to be opened in 1270, and we believe that they have been sealed since the completion of the east wall in 1120. The placing of the rose might have been a romantic gesture by one of the masons who built the abbey.'

The roses of Romsey are inveterately famous. One of the earliest historical references to a formal flower garden in Britain concerns a visit by William Rufus to Romsey Abbey in 1093.

It says: 'The King entered the cloister as if to inspect the roses and other flowers.' The Romsey rose is young compared with the oldest botanical specimen yet found, a posy recovered from Tutankhamun's tomb. But it is still an extremely important event for paleobotany.

Different conservation treatments are to be tried to discover the most suitable. It may even be possible to revive the seeds so that the old rose blooms again. After its treatment at the Natural History Museum, it will be examined by Dr Melville of the Royal Botanic Gardens at Kew.

13 February 1976

[A fortnight later Mr Stubbs, clearly a master of the art of bathos, declared that the 'flower' was in fact a bulb of some kind, quite probably an onion.]

£400 'LIVING SCULPTURE' DEFENDED

Three graduates in fine arts who were given an Arts Council grant of nearly £400 to walk around East Anglia with a 10-ft yellow pole tied to their heads denied yesterday that it was a waste of money.

Mr Kenneth Weetch, MP for Ipswich, has asked Mr Hugh

Jenkins, minister with responsibility for the arts, to investigate why they were given the grant.

One of the men, Mr Raymond Richards, aged 22, of Trent Boulevard, West Bridgford, Nottingham, said: 'The MP's reaction is narrow-minded. We are not conning people just to get the money. If we had not got the grant we would probably have saved up the money and done it ourselves. It is an attempt to tread new ground in the art world.'

The three men, graduates from Leeds Polytechnic, who walked 150 miles attached to the pole, called the project 'living sculpture'. Most of the grant was spent on living expenses on the journey.

13 March 1976

CHINESE TOLD IT IS RUDE TO STARE AT FOREIGNERS

from David Bonavia

PEKING   Officials of a large Chinese city have been told to mount a campaign to prevent the local people from embarrassing foreigners by following them around in mobs and staring at them. Staring by curious bystanders is one of the biggest tribulations of which foreigners complain in all except three Chinese cities – Shanghai, Peking and Canton.

The inhabitants of those places are so accustomed to the presence of foreigners that they have largely given up the habit of gathering round them to stare and follow them in hundreds, even thousands, when they so much as walk down the street or enter a shop.

After repeated complaints by foreigners, the officials of one large city have issued instructions to prevent this in the future; but so far the indications are that most people there are immune to such injunctions.

The officials were told to put the message across that staring at foreigners is rude, degrading to the Chinese people and disruptive of public order. They cited the instance of an African visitor who left the city prematurely because he could

not bear being stared at (black people suffer worse than most).

In another instance, a Western visitor told his guide that he 'just wanted to go away and hide' when people clustered round to stare at him in a shop.

The official instructions pointed out that Chinese people found foreigners strange because of the different colour of their hair and eyes and their different facial structure. Such curiosity was understandable but was not a sign of friendship. It also showed up the ignorance of Chinese people about the outside world.

Staring, it was stated, also damaged China's status as a counterweight to the 'two superpowers' – the Soviet Union and America – and gave a wrong impression. There were also people who stared at foreigners out of hostility or envy for their bourgeois way of life, and such attitudes were particularly condemned.

It was pointed out that to follow foreigners around in large numbers made things difficult for the police and permitted 'class enemies' to commit acts of theft.

Foreigners in China will be greatly relieved to know that something is being done about this persecution, which makes it almost impossible to go for a quiet stroll in most of China's cities. However, many suspect that the abiding curiosity of the Chinese regarding foreigners will persist for a long time.

19 March 1976

THE PERILS OF A LOVE THAT VANISHED AT FIRST SIGHT

from Patricia Clough

ROME A farmer from Canneto near Pavia, who found, wooed and won his Sicilian bride without seeing her is now offering 1-million lire (about £650) and a free honeymoon to anyone who will marry her instead. The swain's decision came when, after a long courtship by correspondence, he finally set eyes on the girl.

The 28-year-old bridegroom, whose identity has not been disclosed, is one of many young northern farmers who have been unable to find wives because the local girls prefer the easier life in the cities. Like many others he asked a marriage broker to find him a good southern girl who did not mind hard work on the land.

He was found a girl at Canecatti in Sicily who met all requirements except one – she failed to send a photograph of herself 'because there is no photographer in our village'.

The moment of truth came when the girl finally arrived with her family to meet her future husband. Having promised in

197

writing to marry her, the farmer has been warned somewhat menacingly by his would-be in-laws that in Sicilian eyes she is now 'compromised'.

He therefore decided in desperation to seek the only way out and find her another husband himself. So far he has had no offers.

20 May 1976

LAUGHTER IS NO JOKE AT CONFERENCE ON HUMOUR

from Trevor Fishlock

Sex is not, after all, the last frontier for researchers from the world of psycho-this and that to explain us to ourselves. From America, Europe, and Scandinavia a great head-shrinking legion is coming to Cardiff for the International Conference on Humour and Laughter, to see what makes us laugh.

For three intensive days they will have mirth on the couch. The agenda lists 80 lectures and papers.

A guest 'chairperson' sets the tone with a talk called 'Why study humour?' After that, delegates get down to 'phylogenetic and ontogenetic considerations for a theory on the origins of humour', followed by 'Elephants and marshmallows: A theoretical synthesis of incongruity'. Meanwhile, 'Cognitive and disparagement theories of humour: A theoretical and empirical synthesis' is likely to have them in the aisles.

A lecture on 'Mirth measurement' provides a sensible preparation for another called 'Joseph Grimaldi to Charlie Cairoli, a semiotic approach to humour'. But there might be difficulty later when two important lectures clash.

Delegates will have to choose 'Operationalization of incongruity' or 'Companion variables in the appreciation of sexual humour'.

Next day the chairperson introduces the topic of 'humour among au pairs'. Typical of several lectures about juvenile humour is 'Children's application of verbal jokes in relation to conceptual tempo'.

Later, delegates will examine a live specimen, Mr Ken Dodd, the comedian, who will be giving a late-night lecture. He says he represents Knotty Ash University.

The conference, organized by the Welsh branch of the British Psychological Society, is from 13 to 16 July. For some lighter relief, towards the end of the conference, there is a lecturer from France, bringing up *le rire*, so to speak.

2 July 1976

SLOTH MOTH ENIGMA SOLVED

The enigmatic life-history of the sloth moth, a little dark moth which spends its leisurely life on the back of the South American sloth, has been solved by two American biologists. It turns out that the moth regards the sloth as little more than the provider of dung to lay its eggs in, and it rides around on the sloth's back to be at hand when it descends from the trees once a week to deposit a neat pile of dung pellets on the jungle floor.

Dr Jeffrey Waage, from Princeton University, and Dr Gene Montgomery, from the National Zoological Park in Washington, became suspicious of the generally accepted view that the sloth moth spent its whole life from larva to adult on the sloth when nobody could find the slightest trace of eggs or larvae in the fur.

The idea had been that the moth larvae fed on either the fur or the body secretions of the sloth, but when eggs from moths taken from a captured sloth were hatched the larvae would feed only on sloth dung, and not on fur or on leaves from trees that the sloths normally live in. With that clue the biologists were soon able to find the silken tubes spun by the larvae among pellets of sloth dung on the forest floor.

When the larvae are mature they pupate in the dung pile and the adult moth that emerges flies up to the forest canopy to look for a new sloth to live on.

17 July 1976

ANASTASIA: THE REAL FACTS AT LAST

What really happened in that damp cellar in Rekmanswurt in July 1918 when the Bolsheviks held the Russian royal family prisoner? Investigations involving some of the most frequently and elaborately crowned heads of Europe have proved inconclusive. But now two former BBC journalists, P. H. Simpligessverk and Justow Serious, have unearthed a previously undisclosed dossier, which they bought remarkably cheaply from a chap called Keating in the Portobello Road, and which strongly reinforces the uncertainty surrounding the case. Next week they will tell you the really interesting bits but this week, in case any of you did not see the film, they retell the remarkable yet inconclusive story of the woman who claims to be the real Anastasia:

She lives today in a tree-lined Wates estate near Watford. The door was opened by Dr Auberon Worsthorne, lecturer in Impending Holocaust at the Open University, who married Anastasia thinking she might be a valuable weapon in the class war that is to come. The wall is hung with empty vodka bottles but the most interesting decorative feature is on the balcony, where a plastic bath is filled with recumbent journalists, bound and gagged, who have incurred the Grand Duchess's wrath.

'She has mixed feelings about journalism', Worsthorne explained. 'Sometimes she refuses to see them even if they have come from as far afield as Uxbridge. And some she keeps out there in case there is a shortage this winter. But she does not take against them all and I think you are lucky.'

Anastasia, a frail, diminutive figure in a veil and plastic raincoat, spoke for the first time. 'Samovar best friends are journalists,' she quipped, showing that despite her tribulations she retains an impish wit. She aimed a playful kick at her pet mink, trying to climb into Worsthorne's trousers.

Journalistically it was an unrewarding evening. In 18 hours of conversation perhaps five minutes were devoted to the question of her identity. But in her rare moments of lucidity she managed to tell how she escaped from Rekmanswurt and, crossing the border at Chalfont St Petersburg, she reached

Emelempstad, where she married a cleansing engineer, who disappeared during the siege of Princesrizburg.

She then fell into the appalling company of Count 'Squirrel' Nutkin, who used falsified documents to establish her identity, in order to claim her share of the Tsarist fortune, believed to be in a secret numbered account at the Trustee Savings Bank. The forgery was exposed by Princess Geraldine Normanov, Anastasia's cousin, since when the Grand Duchess has earned her living playing bit parts in *Upstairs, Downstairs*.

Other members of the Normanov family have offered conflicting evidence. Prince Magnusson, cousin of the Tsarina, asked her 14 questions, all of which she answered correctly, winning a place in the final.

The evidence remained tantalizingly inconclusive until the end of our long interview. As we left to go, she asked gnomically: 'Do you really want a story?' Then she ripped off her veil and revealed an aristrocratic face with a bushy black moustache.

'Lord Lucan!' we exclaimed simultaneously. Thus the question of who is the real Anastasia remains inconclusively tantalizing. That will not, however, stop sharp operators like ourselves from writing books about it, picking up useful sums of money from serialization rights, etc.

7 September 1976

WHY LOBSTERS MOVE IN QUEUES

Spiny lobsters, alone of their genus, migrate across the seafloor tail-to-antenna, in orderly queues. That peculiar behaviour, according to biologists in Florida, probably evolved as a means of reducing the drag of the surrounding water and enabling the animals to move faster.

During autumnal mass migrations, spiny lobsters (*Palinurus argus*) may travel for several days in queues of up to 65 animals, maintaining contact with each other by means of their antennae. Dr R. G. Bill and Dr W. F. Herrnkind, of Florida State University, watched and photographed them in their natural habitat in Bimini, Bahamas, and found that well formed queues could move at a speed of 35 centimetres a second. That compared with 28 centimetres a second for individuals moving alone.

To investigate the cause of that advantage, the biologists measured the drag on preserved specimens of spiny lobsters, towed through a tank of water. By means of a capstan, pulley and weighted pendulum they measured the drag both on individuals and on queues held together by stainless steel wire.

The outcome was that drag was less for queues than for individual lobsters, and the difference increased as speed increased. For example, at 35 centimetres a second a queue of 19 preserved lobsters registered 65 per cent less drag than the 19 towed individually. Drag was greater if the antennae were spread out than if they were close together. There was also an optimal distance between lobsters, for which drag was at a minimum.

Dr Bill and Dr Herrnkind point out that the behaviour of migrating spiny lobsters takes full advantage of drag reduction, thus conserving their energy as much as possible. Queues split and rejoin during migration, so that different lobsters occupy the leading position where drag is greatest. By maintaining contact through their antennae the lobsters keep themselves spaced at the optimal distance.

Since spiny lobsters are the only lobsters known to form queues while migrating, it seems that they must have had some special need to increase the efficiency of their movement. Dr Bill and Dr Herrnkind suggest that, as well as its effects on drag, queuing could give added protection from predators, but, as they say, it will be more difficult to examine that experimentally.

15 September 1976

[This bizarre scientific report was used a few days later by Bernard Levin as the basis for his article 'The Lobsters are Coming, the Lobsters are Coming'. It appears to have awakened in him a new interest in science – his later preoccupation with the mating habits of the mosquito may be cited as an example. He writes with evident delight of the scientists' use of a stainless steel wire to hold the dummy specimens together ('there's posh you are!'), though he seems to have some difficulty in remembering the names of the scientists – referring to them in one instance as 'old Doc Loony and his mate Frankenstein'.]

FRENCH TRAMP THROWS £1,200 PARTY FOR FRIENDS

LILLE   Lucien Grawier, aged 42, a well-known local tramp, was without a crust of bread or a glass of even the cheapest red wine last Wednesday when he took a casual job as a rag-and-bone man for a local firm.

He was emptying a dustbin of old magazines when out fell a bundle of 100-france (£12) notes pinned together. He counted a hundred of them and instantly stopped work.

Calling on a dozen fellow tramps, he spent the next three days and nights drinking away his fortune. After he passed the last note over the counter, he managed to reach the local police station to report his 'find'. No charge was made and today Lucien was sleeping off a giant hangover.

26 October 1976

AMUSEMENT PARK 'DUMMY' WAS A CORPSE

LONG BEACH, CALIFORNIA   A dummy hanging by a noose at the Long Beach Pike Amusement Park has turned out to be a corpse.

The figure had been part of a 'fun house' exhibit for five years. Officials at the park discovered that it was a corpse during the filming of an episode of the *Six Million Dollar Man* television show.

A film crewman was adjusting the arm of the dummy when it fell off. On examination a protruding bone was noted and he identified the dummy as a human body.

Authorities described the corpse as an elderly man, 5 ft 3 in. tall and weighing 159 lb, but could not say when he died.

The figure, wrapped in gauze and sprayed with fluorescent paint, had been bought by the amusement park from a local wax museum, according to the *Los Angeles Times*.

Officials from the coroner's office said the body was well-preserved 'like a mummy and quite leathery'.

10 December 1976

UGANDA OFFER TO MR HEATH 'AND BAND'

President Amin announced tonight that he has invited Mr Edward Heath, the former Prime Minister, to fly to Uganda 'with his band' to play before him during celebrations to mark the anniversary of the military coup that brought him to power.

The President's telegram says he understands that Mr Heath has been 'demoted to the obscure rank of music band-master' but adds that he also understands Mr Heath is one of the best 'bandmasters' in Britain.

He offers either to send air tickets for Mr Heath and his 'band', or to provide a Ugandan aircraft.

Expressing sympathy for Britain's economic difficulties, he offers to assist Mr Heath with a supply of goats, chickens and agricultural produce.

11 January 1977

TOO LATE

Camden borough librarian Frank Cole has just received in the post, 39 years late, a suggestion form dated 14 July 1938, issued by the old Hampstead public libraries. It is signed by J. Fortescue Brown, living in Hampstead, and declares: 'I suggest that all these disgusting books by Havelock Ellis and similar dirty-minded men posing as psychiatrists be removed from your shelves.

'One of the best bandmasters in Britain . . .'
[UGANDA OFFER TO MR HEATH AND BAND]

'Nay, sir; I do more than suggest it – I demand it! You are contributing to the undoubted undermining of the fibre of the English people – and if war comes, as it most certainly will, we shall be in no fit state to wage it.'

5 April 1977

KING DAVID CLEARED OF MASSACRING PRISONERS

by Philip Howard

King David has been a controversial figure for the 30 centuries since he slept with his fathers and was succeeded by Solomon. But he has finally been cleared and rehabilitated from one of the graver charges against him, that of massacring his prisoners-of-war by torture.

The charge is made in a peculiarly gruesome verse in the Old Testament, 2 Samuel 12:31. David is said to have taken the vanquished citizens of Rabbath Ainmon (modern Amman in Jordan) 'and put them under saws, and under harrows of iron, and under axes of iron, and made them pass through the brick-kiln'.

Modern commentaries and translations, including the influential Revised Standard Version (1952) and the New English Bible (1970), ingeniously amend the text to exonerate David from that savage war crime: 'He set them to work with saws and other iron tools, sharp and toothed, and made them work in the brick-kilns' (NEB).

In a paper read to the Glasgow University Orientalist Society, Dr John Sawyer, of Newcastle University, has argued persuasively that there is no justification for those emendations, and that they are due to a misunderstanding of the nature and purpose of the text. In all probability David did not torture the Ammonites or burn them alive in his brick-kilns, but the evidence is to be found not in the naive assumption that 'David could not have done such a thing', but in the language of the text.

In the first place, the terms used for 'saw' and 'brick-kiln' are of a different type, grammatically and semantically, from the terms translated 'harrow' and 'axe'. The first two occur in the singular (collective) form, and are both precise technical terms, associated with building operations. The other two occur in the plural, do not have a precise technical usage, are qualified by the term 'iron', and carry identifiable associations with killing and torture (cf. Amos 1:3).

The grammatical forms of the two verbs translated 'put' and 'pass' are also different. The first is normal in classical Hebrew prose, the second is normal in later Hebrew. The second verb also has overtones of brutality, in particular as a term applied to human sacrifice: for example, 'he made his son pass through the fire' (2 Kings 21:6).

Accordingly, it looks very much as though the original neutral report stated that 'David set them to work with stone-cutting saws and brick-making implements'; and that at a later stage that was reinterpreted, and the three emotive terms referring to torture and killing were added.

9 May 1977

BUSINESS DIARY

The following bitter-sweet observation comes from a statement by the Bavarian farmers' union: 'God's Ten Commandments contain (in German) 279 words and the American Declaration of Independence 300. The European Community's ordinance on the import of caramel sweets has exactly 25,911.'

9 May 1977

WORM'S EYE VIEW OF VENICE

VENICE   Millions of reddish-green worms have suddenly surfaced in the Grand Canal and no one knows why. A museum official said they had never been seen before in the centre of Venice.

18 May 1977

CHILD SAVED WITH THE HELP OF AGATHA CHRISTIE

by John Roper

A nurse who was reading an Agatha Christie thriller indirectly saved the life of a severely ill child whose condition baffled doctors at Hammersmith Hospital, London, it was learnt yesterday.

One Sunday morning a girl, aged 19 months, flown to England from Qatar, was admitted to the hospital semiconscious and unresponsive to speech or commands.

All the resources of the hospital were used to establish a diagnosis, but doctors were at a loss.

The child's condition seemed to decline. Her blood pressure suddenly increased, she became more moribund, and the use of a respirator machine was considered. The decision was difficult because there was no firm diagnosis. Happily, her breathing improved spontaneously.

The next day at the routine ward round, Marsha Maitland, the nurse with particular responsibility for the child, put down the book she was reading and interrupted the doctors' discussion with a suggestion that the child seemed to have thallium poisoning.

The doctors were surprised. Nurse Maitland said that in *A Pale Horse*, the Agatha Christie book she was reading, thallium poisoning was described, and the child's symptoms were remarkably similar. The one consistent feature emphasized in the book, loss of hair, seemed to be developing in the child that morning.

The doctors listened. Thallium poisoning was not one of the toxic substances screened in the laboratory tests and the laboratory, in answer to a request, said that they were unable to carry it out.

Advice was sought from Scotland Yard, which had the address of a laboratory which would test for thallium poisoning. The Yard told the doctors they had an expert living near them: Graham Young, serving life imprisonment at Wormwood Scrubs, next door to the hospital. He, the Yard said, had kept meticulous notes throughout his studies on the effects of thallium.

The laboratory test showed that the child's body contained more than 10 times the permitted maximum of thallium. A reappraisal of her condition showed white Mee's lines on her fingernails and hair showing a dark band of thallium deposition.

Inquiries from the child's parent suggested that the most likely source of the thallium, probably ingested by the child over a long period, was a domestic poison commonly used where she lived to kill cockroaches and rodents.

Although the prognosis, once neurological symptoms have set in, is usually thought to be hopeless, the child was treated and after three weeks was obviously recovering. She was discharged and after four months had improved remarkably.

23 June 1977

BANK'S $999,000 SUIT AGAINST FILIPINO COUPLE

MANILA   Because of a clerical error Mellon Bank, of Pittsburgh, Pennsylvania, has remitted $1m (£560,000) to a Filipino couple who were supposed to receive $1,000. The bank is now suing the couple, Mr Melahor Javier and his wife, Victoria, to recover $999,000. The Javiers claim that most of the amount has been irretrievably spent and say the remaining money will not be returned unless Mellon Bank withdraws the suit.

Instead of returning the money, the Javiers transferred the amount into a dollar account except for about $24,000.

1 August 1977

PSYCHO-FOLK'S FANCY TURNS TO THE RECIPROCITY OF AMORANT FEELING

from Trevor Fishlock

Barbara Cartland, you should be in Swansea at this hour. That dreamy, honey-fed, borne-on-gossamer-wings feeling that your heroines know as love is laid out naked on the couch for the inspection of 200 psychologists and other psycho-people and 40 members of the world's press in their capacity of guardians of the public interest.

The head-shrinking legion has flown in from 12 countries to debate what happens when boy meets girl. They whisper sweet nothings to each other in their dreadful jargon, psycho-ese. They do not talk of love, but of amorance, which they define as the cognitive-affective state characterized by intrusive and obsessive fantasizing concerning reciprocity of amorant feeling by the object of the amorance, or OA.

The delegates have gathered for the first international conference on love and attraction. They feel that the development of work on aspects of human sexuality requires a great comparing of notes. After all, almost everyone is interested in love and sex to some extent, and the waiting rooms, bedsitters and agony columns are full of people with love and sex troubles. In pushing back the frontiers of science the psycho-folk leave no cranny unexplored. Thus they are hearing talks on 'personality characteristics of the average rubber fetishest', a consumer's view of sex therapy, and 'seductive behaviour in hospitalized persons', which concludes that sexual expression is curtailed when a person enters hospital.

Some delegates are especially looking forward to a talk on unmarried cohabitation in Sweden and mate selection in Holland.

7 September 1977

BITTEN MAN MAY BE CHARGED

A man whose nose was bitten by a crocodile may be charged under the Dangerous Animals Act.

The jaws of the 2-ft reptile had to be prised apart in a bookshop at West Bromwich, where the injured man and a companion had taken the crocodile for a walk.

21 September 1977

HITCH SERVICE

Those motorists who are normally disinclined to draw up on the slip roads of motorway service stations to oblige hitch-hikers whose cards bear such legends as 'Birmingham' and 'Bristol' must none the less have admired the initiative of a young soldier waiting at Scratchwood service station on the M1. His card read: 'Treat yourself to the luxury of a personal military escort.'

7 December 1977

CHINA MAY HAVE SEEN THE STAR OF BETHLEHEM

by Clifford Longley

The star of Bethlehem, hitherto known only from the second chapter of St Matthew, has come back to light as a result of a search by Three Wise Men from the West through the pages of ancient Chinese and Korean astronomical records.

They were looking for long-past heavenly happenings in the hope of finding something interesting to observe: they found reports of a sudden bright star just about in the right place at the right time to have been the star of Matthew 2:2.

The three are astronomers: Mr John Parkinson of the Mullard Space Science Laboratory, Dorking; Mr Richard Stephenson, of Newcastle University; and Mr David Clark, of the Royal Greenwich Observatory. Mr Clark, a New Zealander, has worked at the Anglo-Australian telescope in Australia, and it was his interest in mapping the southern constellations that led them to Chinese and Korean documents.

In a paper in the December edition of the *Quarterly Journal of the Royal Astronomical Society* they explain that Far Eastern astronomers were the best in the world two thousand years ago. If something strange did occur in the skies at that time they would almost certainly have seen it and recorded it.

Some of those records have been translated and republished, and a search of those available produced two positive sightings. In the Astronomical Treatise of the History of the Former Han Dynasty (the *Ch'ien-han-shu*), they found the entry: 'Second year of the Ch'ien-p'ing reign period, second month, a hui-hsing appeared at Ch'ien-niu for over 70 days.'

As it was apparently stationary it cannot have been a comet, and the period for which it was observed would be typical of a nova, a so-called new star that is in fact a runaway thermonuclear explosion on the surface of a white dwarf in a binary system.

* * *

212

It seems that only astronomers in the Far East would have been interested, as those elsewhere, particularly in the Middle East, were far more concerned with the solar system and the movements of the planets. That explains why there are no other Western reports of a sudden bright object, they conclude.

Mr John Parkinson said yesterday that theirs was the first piece of original astronomical research on the subject for many years. Novae, which are less catastrophic than super-novae, do sometimes recur, which raises the fascinating possibility that the star of Bethlehem might one day come back.

13 December 1977

HANDLE WITH CAUTION

A letter from the Devil to all his disciples and dated 'apud centrum terrae in nostro pallacio tenebroso', is obviously to be treated with caution. Sotheby's took no chances when they sold one, together with a group of medieval moral tracts, yesterday. The catalogue states that it is 'not, apparently, autograph, but cf. A. N. L. Munby, *The Alabaster Hand*, 1950, pp. 181–2 and 192'. I think that one should.

15 December 1977

[Munby's *Alabaster Hand* describes an elderly dabbler in the black arts, seen through the eyes of his nephew. The old man vanishes mysteriously, but a letter, whose opening words are those quoted here, is found in his study. The letter is written in a bold hand, 'in red ink, or so I thought at the time – though later another possibility occurred to me'.]

COOPERMAN BY ANY OTHER NAME

from Michael Leapperson

A judge in the New York state Supreme Court has, after three years of litigation, allowed the former Mrs Ellen Cooperman

213

to call herself Ellen Cooperperson. His ruling reversed that of a lower court last year when a judge called the proposed new name inane and nonsensical.

In 1974 Mrs Cooperman (as she then was), a film producer, divorced Mr Norman Cooperman and decided to alter her surname on the grounds that the old one was sexist. She began legal moves, normally a formality, only to have the petition rejected last year.

In granting her new petition yesterday, Justice Leon Lazer said that she had a right in law to adopt a name of her own choosing, so long as it would not lead to fraud, evasion or to misleading others. There was no reason to think it would do any of those things.

Mrs Cooperperson said that last year's rejection of her petition provoked much sympathy from people who would not normally be regarded as keen supporters of women's liberation. Her 10-year-old son Brian would keep the name Cooperman, she added, because he was male and thus not uncomfortable with it.

17 December 1977

[A few months later, however, the Woonsocket, Rhode Island, council were reported to be fighting back: in a 'sudden about face' the councillors had dropped a proposal to rename the town's manholes 'personholes'.]

JUDGE SAYS NO TO MR 1069

MINNEAPOLIS   A judge has ruled that Mr Michael Herbert Dengler cannot change his name to 1069, because a number 'is totalitarian and an offence to human dignity'.

Mr Dengler, a former social studies teacher, said he wanted to be called 1069 because the number 'symbolized his inter-relationship with society and reflected his personal and philosophical identity'. He said each digit had significance for him.

15 February 1978

MR FELIX FAILS TO BUY LONDON STATION

by Alan Hamilton

The British Railways Board has declined, perhaps with a tinge of regret, an offer from Mr Jennings P. Felix, of Seattle, Washington, to buy Victoria Station, London, and turn it into an antique market.

Mr Felix, senior partner in the law firm of Felix and Zimmer, attorney and counsellors, who had gained the impression that the terminus might be for sale, wrote to the Department of Trade and offered to send representatives to Britain to complete the deal. In his letter Mr Felix said he was acting for Antique World Inc. and Antique World, of Kansas City, Missouri, Inc., two companies that have taken over railway stations and converted them to antique stores.

The potential buyer did not make clear whether he wanted to leave the station on its present site in SW1 or to dismantle it brick by brick and reconstruct it in the Arizona desert. What he did make clear was that his offer was not to be regarded as an idle joke.

The Department of Trade passed the letter to Southern Region, whose estates surveyor passed it on to the British Rail Property Board with the not entirely serious observation that it appeared a unique opportunity to dispose of this troublesome edifice once and for all.

But the property board, for which the sale of 21 acres of prime real estate in the City of Westminster would be a notable coup, is about to reply to Mr Felix, through the British Consul in Seattle, that Victoria is unfortunately still required for handling trains.

Why the American antique station collectors thought that Victoria was on the market is unclear. Certainly British Rail has been toying for some years with grand plans for a reconstruction of the terminus, but in the light of reality has settled for a face lift and a £40m resignalling scheme. The concourse is being enlarged, a new ticket office has been built, and the interior is being cleaned.

Not even British Rail would argue with the desirability of

selling off Victoria and building a better station in its place. The present terminus is an unhappy hotch-potch of two separate stations, one built for the South Eastern and Chatham Railway and the other for the London, Brighton and South Coast line. Many of the 171,000 passengers who use it daily would regard plans to convert it to an antique market as superfluous.

As antiques go, the eighth largest and second busiest station in Britain is a modern upstart, not even Victorian in spite of its name, built between 1901 and 1908 to replace an earlier station on the site.

If the American collectors want a real antique to add to Seattle and Kansas City they should go for Brunel and Wyatt's magnificent structure of 1854 at Paddington, Lewis Cubitt's avant-garde frontage of 1851 at King's Cross, or Sir George Gilbert Scott's 1868 Gothic extravaganza at St Pancras, soon to be cleaned and restored to its original splendour.

9 March 1978

VICTORIA'S UNDERWEAR FROM UNNAMED SOURCE IS SOLD

by Geraldine Norman

Some of Queen Victoria's underclothes were offered for sale by Bonham's yesterday. A pair of knee-length drawers, of fine linen with three rows of pin-tucks around the bottom of each voluminous leg, and a linen chemise, the short sleeves edged with lace, made £185 (estimate £125 to£175) to Gaughin from America. Both are embroidered with the royal cipher.

The same buyer spent £50 on a lawn handkerchief embroidered with the royal monogram and a black muff trimmed with ostrich feathers believed to have belonged to Queen Victoria but not bearing the royal cipher.

Granny's Attic, a Suffolk dealer, paid £110 (estimate £40 to £70) for two pairs of stockings. One pair is black silk and the other pale pink but each stocking bears the royal cipher. A white huckaback hand towel with the initials 'VRI' and the date 1899 finely embroidered in red in one corner made £20 (estimate £10 to £15).

This is the fourth occasion on which Bonham's have had Queen Victoria's intimate garments for sale from an unnamed source.

8 April 1978

THE CASE OF THE UNINVITED GUEST

A caterpillar was found in a tin of Spanish tomatoes, so the canteen management at United Yeast in Morden, Surrey, sent a letter of complaint to the canning factory in Murcia. They received the following reply: 'Tins are running for a line with plenty hot water til were the women are doing the selection of tomatoes, when the cans arrive there and to take off the hot water that maybe you can fine in, the same line turn-off the tins so everything inside go out. One tins arrive then women full it by hand, mens tomato by tomato, so is impossible to get any foreing matter into any of our tins but if women do not so a proposal, thing that is unbelieve.' Which tells United Yeast everything except how the caterpillar got into the tomatoes.

3 May 1978

STATION VINES WILL NOT BE DISTURBED

Vines growing on the Victorian railway station at Knebworth, Hertfordshire, will not be disturbed when the building is demolished to make way for a new one.

British Rail has decided to build round them. In recent summers commuters have been able to pick grapes while waiting for trains, and station staff produced a homemade wine.

20 June 1978

HOW TO TELL THE REAL GENTLEMEN OF ENGLAND

by Philip Howard

The English gentleman, a species previously supposed as dead as the dodo, is resurrected today in a book from Debrett's Peerage. The stud book to the upper classes for the past two centuries is branching out as a social arbiter, with books on every aspect of etiquette and gentlemanly behaviour.

The first blast in this monstrous regimen of snobbery, entitled *The English Gentleman*, is published today. It takes a defiantly old-fashioned and whimsical view of its endangered species, with much emphasis on clubs and nannies, shooting and hunt balls.

Its author, Major Douglas Sutherland, lives in one of the coldest little castles in Scotland, where society changes more slowly, and the gent is still a protected species.

According to Debrett's, a gentleman always has highly polished shoes, carries his handkerchief tucked in his sleeve, and, if he is traditionally minded, smokes his cigar with the band on, a habit he shares with bookmakers.

He has only two suits, one for funerals, and one for going up to London; but innumerable jackets, mostly patched with leather. He lives in a country house (Surrey does not qualify as country) filled with Victorian furniture. When anything wears out it is replaced with something older, usually Regency, from the attic. So his furniture gets better and better.

On that handkerchief, Debrett's parts company with Nancy Mitford, that other mischievous arbiter of U and non-U. Miss Mitford ruled that a gentleman wore a handkerchief carefully arranged in his top pocket and another somewhere else on his person. Major Sutherland describes that principle of one for show and one for blow as being as middle-class and Non-U as a lady who carries her handkerchief tucked in the elastic of her knickers.

10 July 1978

PLEASE HELP

The friendly little verb 'to help' is being rapidly worsened so as to become distinctly unfriendly. For some time a man said to be helping the police with their inquiries has been understood not to be lending a hand to the hard-pressed police out of voluntary benevolence as a good citizen. The euphemism is taken to mean that he is being interrogated, his arrest imminent, and subsequent conviction probable.

Now the amiable little question 'Can I help you?' shows alarming signs of acquiring an aggressive ring. Snarled in its now-customary tone of voice it can be translated as 'What the hell are you doing here? And can I help you out of here as quickly as possible?' A similar deterioration is affecting 'please'. In many contexts and tones of voice it is now ruder to say please than to leave it out. Compare 'Just a moment' and 'Just a moment, please'. The full 'if you please' is even ruder. These developments may be part of our fashionable modern horror of sounding patronizing or even educated. At this rate it will not be long before 'thank you' becomes an insult, and 'sorry' a malediction.

15 August 1978

DOCTOR TIES UP HIS CLAIM TO FAME

by Philip Howard

There is only a limited number of ways of tying a knot. Although the man who has just knotted his shoelace, or the fisherman who has just narled his cast into an inextricable tangle, may find it hard to believe, it is rare for a new knot to be invented.

Dr Edward Hunter, a retired consultant physician, has just done it. His knot, Hunter's Bend, is about to be published in the specialist journals that interest themselves in knotty matters in Britain and the United States.

In the implicative and convoluting world inventing a knot is the equivalent of discovering a comet. Dr Hunter is about to join the select company, stretching from Gordius (the Phrygian peasant who became a king) to Matthew Walker (single or double) who have achieved immortality by becoming eponyms of the knots they invented.

Hunter's Bend has the following characteristics. It is stronger than the sheet bend or the Fisherman's bend. It is easily tied and untied. It is suitable for tow-ropes, thin nylon, and for ropes of different sizes.

To tie it (in the words of inventor): Lay the two ropes parallel, with the ends opposite; throw a bight (loop) on the double (overlapping) part; tuck the ends through the bight in opposite directions; and a pull on the standing parts will draw it snug.

Inspector Geoffrey Budworth, of the Metropolitan Police, a leading authority on knots and part-time consultant to the National Maritime Museum on the subject, said yesterday: 'Dr Hunter has either discovered a new bend not recognized in the literature, or rediscovered something that has dropped out of our knowledge.

'You can invent esoteric and clumsy knots that are useless. Hunter's Bend is good because it has a distinct shape, is stable, does not distort, is readily untied, and does not reduce the breaking strain of the line. It is a useful addition to the repertoire of people who still use knots.'

The last important knot to be invented was the Tarbuck knot, first tied 20 years ago by Ken Tarbuck, a climber, for use with ropes of man-made fibre. It is still used for attaching the last man to a string of climbers.

The inventor and eponym, Dr Hunter, has in his time been a missionary in Nigeria, where he was caught up in the Biafran war, a ship's surgeon, and a consulting physician.

He has interested himself in knots for many years, and carves knots that can be undone out of wood. He said yesterday: 'There is great intellectual pleasure in knots. They have an intricacy and satisfaction similar to those of crosswords.'

6 October 1979

DOLPHINS FEAR CRY OF GLASS FIBRE WHALE

from Peter Hazelhurst

TOKYO   The prototype of a mechanical killer whale, designed to frighten dolphins away from Japan's fishing waters, appears to deceive the ocean's most intelligent mammal, when recorded cries of the whale are transmitted from within the equipment.

The black and white glass fibre model of a killer whale was tested for the first time yesterday. It was towed close to 15 dolphins, trapped in an enclosure in the bay of Taiji, near the southern tip of Honshu island.

At first the dolphins ignored the life-sized model of their feared natural enemy as it sidled up to the pen with its dorsal fin above the water.

Then engineers switched on recordings of the ferocious cries of the killer whale, magnified a hundredfold by electronic equipment, deep within the mechanical beast's fibre glass head.

When the plaintive deep bass cry of the killer whale echoed through the water, the dolphins showed immediate signs of insecurity. Squeaking in apparent panic, the 15 mammals grouped together, lashing the water into white foam as they swam round in a tight circle.

The cries of the killer whale were recorded in an aquarium in Toronto. Officials said the cries were expected to impress the dolphins because the recordings were made while the killer whale was hungry and searching for food.

As the model glided past the pen the electronic device was switched off and the mammals appeared to relax.

Mr Shinichi Yajima, an official in charge of the research programme, said: 'They showed discernible signs of panic when the cries were turned on, but they were not perturbed by the silent model.'

The mechanical whale was constructed at a cost of £8,500. The project was begun when the slaughter of 1,000 dolphin by

'. . . showed discernible signs of panic'
[DOLPHINS FEAR CRY OF GLASS FIBRE WHALE]

Japanese fishermen off the island of Iki this year led to an international outcry.

Taken aback by the protests from Europe and the United States, Mr Takeo Fukuda, the Prime Minister, called for research to establish whether dolphin could be driven away from fishing grounds by more acceptable methods.

After eight months of work at the fishing agency's research laboratory the initial stage of the experiment appears to be successful.

The laboratory is now attempting to record distress signals of the dolphin. A scientist said: 'If we can achieve this it will cause double panic.'

30 November 1978

[On 4 August 1981 it was reported that Soviet scientists, reversing this idea, were using mechanical dolphins to frighten Pacific herrings away from rivers where their eggs would die. But the first recorded practical deployment of glass fibre fish was on 12 May 1976, when a glass fibre shark was tested on the Isis river. In this case the robot was designed to frighten humans – its purpose being to keep trippers away from millionaires' beaches.]

No editions of The Times appeared between 30 November 1978 and 13 November 1979.

JAPANESE TAUGHT DEFERENCE IN BOWING MACHINE

It is not enough to just bow in Japan. The exact angle of the bow must be determined by the nuances and subtle shades of a complex system of social intercourse.

But today, as the country continues to absorb the ways of the West, older Japanese are worried that the new generation is losing the gentle art of bowing. And so, with a penchant for precision which has turned the country into an economic power, the Japanese have now invented the great bow training machine.

Called the *ojigi renshuki* (literally translated the bow training machine) the device was first developed by Mr Takahashi Torimoto and a research team from the Kintetsu company, one of Osaka's largest chain of department stores.

Retailed at a price of £150, the machine consists of a stand, a breast plate and a complex system of swivels and dials. A student of the refined bow stands upright in the machine with his chest against the breast plate. The plate then lowers the top half of the torso forward to the correct angle for pre-selected conditions on the social scale. Trainees can observe a calibrated dial out of the corner of their eyes.

Mr Takahashi said the machine was first designed to train the Kintetsu company's newly recruited employees to bow correctly to customers, senior supervisors and their peers on the shop floor.

After using the device to train newly recruited staff in May this year the department store has now placed the machine on sale. 'We have applied for a patent for the invention. Up until now the machine has been purchased by hotels, Japanese inns, professional schools and institutions which specialize in the service industry,' Mr Takahashi said.

In the case of the Kintetsu department store the machine is used to train newly recruited staff to tilt their torso forward at the exact angle required to greet customers and colleagues.

'The first angle is 15 degrees. This is the angle to be used when bowing to colleagues or a customer in the hallway. The second angle is 30 degrees. This is used when welcoming customers into the store. They are also trained to bow at 45 degrees. This is the angle which is used when a customer departs from the store,' Mr Takahashi said.

'We found that young people no longer know how to bow correctly and it is difficult to explain the form verbally. It can only be done physically so we put them in the machine during their orientation course.'

Like most Japanese Mr Takahashi is modest about his achievements. 'I did not invent the bowing machine by myself. We did it together. The credit must go to the Kintetsu department store.'

24 November 1979

THOMAS CRAPPER FAILS TO WIN A PLAQUE

A suggestion that a blue plaque should be erected to commemorate a former home of the Victorian sanitary engineer, Thomas Crapper, after earnest consideration has been rejected by the historic buildings committee of the Greater London Council.

The committee decided that 'memorable though Crapper's name might be in popular terms', evidence from the Patents Office showed that he was not a notable inventor or pioneer in his field.

27 November 1979

CASE OF BARBER'S CALENDAR GOES TO POPE

from Peter Nichols

Somewhere amid the post arriving for the Pope in the wake of the Kung affair is a letter from a Sardinian barber calling for the Pontiff's intervention in the dispute which has halted the baptism of his best friend's son.

The child is now eight months old, which is an indication of how long the dispute has so far lasted. The barber, Signor Mario Tegas, was chosen by the baby's parents to be godfather. But Don Pietrino Pani, the local priest of Talana, near Nuoro, refused the barber on the grounds that he had a calendar in his shop containing a photograph of a nude woman.

The barber has since removed the calendar but the priest remains obdurate.

The reply to the priest of this pastoral community of 1,500 people was reported to be: 'Remember there are people here who for months see nothing but goats.'

The barber used to work at Orgosolo, the town known as the cathedral of Sardinian banditry, and some of his former clients there offered to come over and help him sort out the trouble.

He refused their offer on the grounds that he wished to use only peaceful means.

22 December 1979

[Kung was the theologian at Tubingen University who had got into hot water with the Sacred Congregation for the Doctrine of the Faith in Rome for 'departing from the integral truth' on Infallibility and other matters. Fr Edward Schillebeeckx, OP, of Nijmegen University had been summoned to Rome for similarly unorthodox views a few weeks before, and both were eventually dismissed, to the accompaniment of much earnest heart-searching and learned discussion, not to mention some very critical comments from both inside and outside the Catholic Church. The earthy moral problems of Talana would presumably have made a welcome change of pace for Vatican officials.]

FLORENTINE DEBIT REGISTER OF 1511 WITH BLANK LEAVES TREBLES SALES ESTIMATE

by Geraldine Norman

An unusual item offered for sale at auction yesterday was an early-sixteenth-century Florentine merchant's debit register, sold by Lawrence's of Crewkerne for £580 (estimate £100–£200).

Its attraction lies in that it contains 119 leaves of unused paper, very clean, the ideal material for a picture-faker. The cataloguer points out: 'While a few blanks sometimes occur, a block of paper of this extent, in virtually unmarked condition contemporary with e.g. Wynkyn de Worde, Leonardo da Vinci and Raphael, is almost unobtainable.'

The volume is of folio size, with a contemporary vellum flap binding, the spine being dated 1511. The sheets have a tulip and leaf watermark. It was bought by Sims and Reed, the London book dealers, specialists in art reference books.

Mr Reed said yesterday: 'I do not think I have ever seen so much blank paper. We bought it for stock. We had some eighteenth-century paper a few years ago, which proved very popular.'

15 February 1980

WASHINGTON'S EXOTIC SETS OF FALSE TEETH

George Washington had dentures made from elephants' tusks and lead and the teeth of humans, cows, hippopotami and probably a walrus, but not from wood, a dentist said today.

Dr Reidar Sognnaes, of the University of California here, said that research he had carried out on the first American President produced no evidence that Washington had wooden stumps as teeth, as some people had believed.

Dr Sognnaes, who reported on his findings to a conference of the American Association for Dental Research, said Washington may not have smiled much in portraits, but he had four sets of false teeth.

Studies of parts of the sets, Dr Sognnaes said, showed that some of the teeth were made from the ivory of elephant tusks. Others came from the teeth of hippopotami and were cut into segments and mounted on ivory.

Washington also had teeth from humans, cows and what appeared to be a walrus, Dr Sognnaes added.

Some of Washington's teeth were also made of lead. They were dark and may have looked like wooden stumps, Dr Sognnaes said.

Although ivory is white, it could be stained with coffee, tea and the port wine that Washington was known to like, he added.

He said Washington had two of his own teeth when he became President in 1789 and one was mounted on a denture. Washington also had other human teeth mounted.

22 March 1980

DRUG HELPED PRAYER, NUN CLAIMS

A nun was in jail in the northern Greek town of Patras today after her superior at the Pepolinitsis convent there found her smoking cannabis in her cell.

Sister Flothee, aged 48, is alleged to have grown the drug in the convent garden. She is said to have told police at Patras that she smoked cannabis as it helped her to 'participate' more in her prayers.

She denied planting the drug and maintained that it was 'God's breezes' which blew seeds into the convent. She is to appear in court.

22 August 1980

BOX OF THE APOCALYPSE

Those already infuriated or depressed by the ubiquity of wall-to-wall music will be less than delighted to learn that in Greater Manchester there are confident expectations that it will trump the Last Trump. A notice seen by a colleague in a hotel bar there proclaims: 'Juke box will be turned off ten minutes after the end of time.'

3 September 1980

KNIFE AND FORK BANK THREAT

WOLLONGONG, AUSTRALIA   Harry Fitchett, aged 59, was accused in court here yesterday of trying to rob a bank with a knife and fork.

Two bank cashiers said Mr Fitchett walked into the bank brandishing the cutlery and demanded money. He was found not guilty of demanding money with menaces.

1 October 1980

'Mr Fitchett . . . demanded money'
[KNIFE AND FORK BANK THREAT]

FUGITIVES ENLIST AID OF TIGERS TO LOSE THEIR PURSUERS

from Richard Hughes

Hongkong's efforts to stem illegal immigration from China have revealed a curious new trade which has developed in the past six months: the sale of tiger's dung.

This, it seems, has become a successful dog repellent, the smell of which can be used to scare away bloodhounds used by Chinese Army units to track and pursue fugitives.

A group of young Chinese in Canton early this year decided to experiment with tiger dung in their escape attempt and, it is reported, discovered that discreet scattering of the substance, sneaked from the city zoo, made the hounds keep a respectful distance.

The news was swiftly transmitted to Canton after they reached Hongkong and a secret but brisk side-business was promoted by Triad gangs, who were organizing the mounting flood of illegal entrants into Hongkong.

Cantonese security authorities recently arrested some young men caught scraping the cages of tigers in the Canton zoo. Inquiries then uncovered the business which, it has been reported by local Kuomintang agents, had expanded into tiger-dung trafficking with rural residents of Hunan and Kwangsi provinces.

Prices reputedly ranged from the equivalent of £4 to £8 a basket. However, risky adulteration of pure tiger dung has become common. 'Pure for the rich illegals and adulterated for the poor', as the Kuomintang report claimed.

28 October 1980

PALAEOLITHIC RECORD OF PREHISTORIC RHYTHM

from Michael Binyon

Melodiya, the Soviet gramophone record company, has just released an unusual recording. An ensemble from Kiev has produced a rhythmic piece of music played on instruments fashioned more than 20,000 years ago from mammoth bones.

The Stone Age instruments, still resounding with a fine timbre, were discovered by archaeologists at a site near Kiev recently.

Six palaeolithic drums, cymbals and other prototype percussion instruments had been carved out of shoulder blade, hip, lower jaw, tusk, shank and skull of a mammoth. They were piled in a ditch.

For some time scientists wondered what they were. They summoned local forensic doctors, restorers from the Hermitage Museum in Leningrad and even criminologists who finally supported the thesis that the old bones were indeed from one of the world's first orchestras.

As proof, they pointd to the smooth parts of the bones where regular drumbeats to produce particular sounds had worn them down. They were at first afraid to try playing the bones in case they shattered at the first blow. But the old fossils were resilient.

The music produced a curiously hypnotic rhythm, which the archaeologists maintain testifies to their use in ritualistic dances and ceremonies round the open fire that followed a successful day's hunting.

Each bone produced a distinctive sound: the tusk was like a xylophone and the skull like a drum. Near the bones were found plate-shaped castinets carved from mammoth tusks which dancers probably wore during the ceremonies.

The Kiev Academy of Sciences decided to allow modern man the chance to listen to his ancestors' favourite hits. After a few experiments with the orchestration, a long-playing record has now been produced and will shortly go on sale in the Soviet Union, *Pravda* announced today. There is indeed music in 'dem dry bones'.

22 November 1980

CHINESE PLAN TO BREED NEAR-HUMAN MONSTER

from David Bonavia

PEKING   The Chinese authorities are considering the renewal of partly successful research on cross-breeding men with chimpanzees to found a strain of helots for economic and technical purposes.

The Shanghai newspaper, *Wen Aui Bao*, said yesterday that a female chimpanzee became pregnant 13 years ago after being inseminated with a man's sperm.

Red Guards, however, smashed up the laboratory and the chimpanzee died, according to Mr Qi Yongxiang, identified only as a 'researcher in medicine', in the north-eastern city of Shenyang.

Mr Qi's ambition is to create what he calls a 'near-human ape'. Through enlargement of its brain and tongue, it should be able to grasp simple concepts and talk some kind of language. Organs from the proposed monster would possibly prove useful as substitutes for human or artificial organs in transplant cases.

It could even drive a car, herd animals, protect forests and natural resources, and be used for exploration of the seabed, outer space and the centre of the Earth.

Asked whether the Earth was not already overpopulated with human beings, let alone hybrids, Mr Qi said that the aim would be to use them for the benefit of humanity.

Asked whether it was ethical to create such a hybrid, Mr Qi said that semen was of no account once it left the body, and could be disposed of like manure. The creature produced would be classed as an animal, so there need be no qualms about killing it when necessary.

11 December 1980

DEEP-FROZEN IMPORTS HELP TO OFFSET FROG-HUNTING BAN

from Ian Murray

France has banned frog hunting. In the interests of protecting the species a near total ban on catching them has been imposed – for the first time – by the Direction de la Protection de la Nature, the French nature conservancy organization.

In its annual publication giving the seasons when fishing for different species is allowed – a complex book which serves as a bible for the sport – the organization rules out catching all but the common or garden pond green frog, or the only slightly less common land red frog.

Even then these two kinds can only be hunted by the families who intend to eat them. Family frog-fishing is permitted, but only in the sort of quantity that a family would be capable of eating.

Other species, in particular the larger green frog with white patches that can be found in meadows, must not be caught in any circumstances.

Restaurateurs are precluded from hunting fresh frogs for their tables, but this will be no hardship to them since nowadays virtually all frog legs on the menu have been deep-frozen in some East European country and imported.

Measures are also being taken to protect the few remaining French sturgeon which still swim in the waters of the Garonne and the Dordogne.

17 December 1980

ODOUR OF ASPARAGUS

A team at Hadassah University Hospital in Jerusalem has concluded, contrary to previous suggestions, that the excretion of uniquely odorous urine after the consumption of asparagus is not a sign of abnormal metabolism.

Several characteristic chemical compounds can be detected in the urine of a person who has recently eaten asparagus, some being held responsible for the characteristic odour. Almost 25 years ago tests revealed one such compound, called methylmercaptan, in the urine of only 46 of 115 subjects who had eaten a large quantity of asparagus.

The cause was attributed to a genetic difference in the way the body deals with asparagus, and the ability to produce methylmercaptan was designated an inherited characteristic. Since then the list of inherited human conditions has included: asparagus, urinary excretion of odoriferous components of.

But to the team in Jerusalem, Dr M. Lison, Dr S. L. Blondheim and Dr R. N. Melmed, that began to seem an inadequate explanation for the differences detected between urines. On the basis of their own observations, they suspected that people differed not in the ability to produce the odour but in the ability to detect it. They followed up their suspicion by testing more than 300 people for their ability to smell the characteristic odour.

Subjects were asked whether they could distinguish the odour in a series of increasing dilutions of urine prepared from a sample collected from a donor a few hours after he had eaten a can of asparagus. Most of the subjects were Israelis who had rarely or never eaten asparagus and had therefore previously been unfamiliar with the odour. The subjects also included 22 Americans, 10 of whom knew they could detect the odour and the rest who could not.

On the basis of their responses to the various dilutions, the subjects could be divided into two groups. One group could distinguish the odour only in the strongest concentrations of urine (the lowest dilutions), whereas the other group, representing about 10 per cent of the subjects, could also detect it in the weaker concentrations. The team denotes that latter group the 'smellers' and the other group, the 'non-smellers'.

The 10 Americans who knew they could detect the odour turned out to be among the smellers, while the other Americans were non-smellers. Furthermore, smellers were able to detect the odour in the urine of anybody who had eaten asparagus, regardless of whether that person could detect it.

From their results, the three scientists conclude that the ability to excrete a characteristically odorous compound (or compounds) after eating asparagus is universal. Their explanation is that people differ in the ability to detect the odour. But whether or not a genetic difference is involved cannot be said.

5 January 1981

HAIGSPEAK REWRITES THE GRAMMAR

from William Safire

A new linguistic form called Haigravation is rearing its head in Washington. It is the tendency of the new Secretary of State to change the state of parts of speech – from noun to adverb, from noun to verb.

The new top man at Foggy Bottom, former General Alexander Haig, studded his testimony at confirmation hearings with locutions such as 'I'll have to caveat my response, senator, and I'll caveat that.'

Caveat, as used by generals like Julius Caesar, is the third-person singular present subjunctive of the Latin *cavere*, to beware. Standing by itself, *caveat* in Latin means 'let him beware'. In English, the word is a noun synonymous with warning. It is also part of the Latin phrase *caveat emptor*, let the buyer beware.

Until now, caveat has been a noun: in Haigravation, it has become a verb: 'I'll caveat that' means, presumably, 'I'll say that with this warning.' (I'll caveat the reader that this locution will soon be followed in literary circles with 'I'll asterisk that'.)

Not to be outdone, Senator John Glenn asked the witness: 'Will you burden-share?' This is a heavy new verb formed from burden-sharing, diplomatic jargon for 'my tax-payers won't kick in any more until yours do'.

But Mr Glenn is not in Mr Haig's verbifying league. 'Not in the way you contexted it, Senator,' was a four-star reply about immorality in high places. To context something, in this lingo, is to place it in context.

Mr Haig has a history of this sort of thing. In hearings last year, the former general said something like: 'There are nuance-al differences between Henry Kissinger and me on

235

that.' The exact quotation cannot be found, because 'nuance-al', or 'nuansle', was expunged from the written record of the hearing by some unknown hand, and 'differences of nuance' put in.

28 January 1981

AN UNGALLANT REWARD FOR MADAME

French justice is ungallant. It has just dished out to a highly respected – if not respectable – woman of 80 a suspended sentence of ten months' imprisonment, and a fine of 250,000 francs (about £24,000) for exercising the oldest profession in the world in an establishment in the residential 16th *arrondissement* of Paris which had a high reputation in its heyday and was frequented by leading personalities of successive regimes.

She was in fact described as the 'pink eminence' of the fourth and fifth republics, and very surprised to find herself in the dock of the Paris police court for infringing a law which since the Liberation has been much more conspicuous in the breach than the observance.

Madame Marie-Louise Soccodato, *née* Roblot, alias 'Madame Billy', said: 'I practised in the full knowledge of the authorities. I worked quietly. The police often came to see me.'

A tax inspector, according to Maitre Ceccaldi, for the defence, even wrote in 1973 that 'the illicit activities of her establishment were notorious . . . Madame Billy is supervised and guided in her activities by the police'.

Her establishment had prospered from 1941 to 1978, and, if the book she published is to be believed, she welcomed within its portals many of distinction in French politics, and quite a few foreign personalities. The Quai d'Orsay even sent her official visitors.

Then why was this spry and smart old lady, perfumed and permed and wrapped in mink, with bejewelled fingers, sitting on the bench of infamy? The Public Prosecutor was not very convincing when he argued that no one had known of her activities.

236

Maitre Ceccaldi said: 'At an investiture of the Legion of Honour, presided over by Valéry Giscard d'Estaing himself, at which Madame Billy was present, she recognized a goodly number of her clients among the guests.

'You say she does not provide any proof of what she maintains, but who would want her to do so, and to have her mention names?' He added to a gale of laughter: 'By prosecuting her, you cast aspersions on the fate which the state reserves to its old and faithful servants.'

24 February 1981

SARDINE LIVING IN OSAKA MINI-HOTEL

from Peter Hazelhurst

If you are over 6 ft tall, suffer from claustrophobia and insist on a good view, then you are advised not to book into the Osaka Capsule Inn.

The advice is provided by Mr Masamitsu Furuichi, manager at the reception desk of Japan's new answer to modern urban living, as he escorts a diminutive guest past tiers of plastic sleeping capsules and invites him to crawl into a tiny room through an entrance resembling the door of a laundromat dryer.

The hotel boasts 411 tiny sleeping capsules, stacked above each other in double banks along the building's dimly-lit corridors. Each capsule is 3 ft high, 30 in. wide and 6 ft deep. They are all self-contained, mini-hotel rooms equipped with reading light, a television set, a radio and a digital alarm clock. Each tiny sleeper is air-conditioned and furnished with a mattress, quilt and newly laundered sheets.

More surprising, the hotel has managed to fill all its capsules every night since it opened two years ago. A night in the Osaka Capsule Inn is cheap simply because its designer, Mr Kisho Kurokawa, a noted architect, has managed to cram four times as many sleeping berths into the area of a small conventional hotel.

The present rate is £5 a night and for £1 extra guests can use the showers, a Japanese bath house and an exotic sauna in the basement. In contrast, conventional local business hotels charge as much as £20 a night while the room rates at many other modern hotels have risen to £50 a night.

Women guests are not accepted. After checking in at the reception desk, patrons can hang up their clothes and deposit their suitcases.

Refreshments can be obtained from vending-machines on each floor of the hotel. A spacious lounge, equipped with comfortable seats and television sets, is located near the lobby.

Mr Koichi Sato, a travelling salesman and a regular patron of the Capsule Inn, says the hotel is popular because it is economical.

'I do not mind being confined in a capsule. I am only using it while I sleep. This means I can use the rest of my travelling allowance for entertainment. I can also save,' he says.

More than 30 per cent of the guests are businessmen who have missed the last train home after a night of drinking.

'It is not as crammed as you might think. Our guests can sit up comfortably in the capsule,' the manager, Mr Furuichi, claims.

He denies the allegations of some guests that the folding screen doors of the capsule fail to contain the sound of loud snores. 'If you put the radio up too loudly, our guests in other capsules might be disturbed. But otherwise they are almost soundproof,' he claims.

Capsule hotels have also sprung up in Nagoya, Tokyo and in Japan's other sprawling urban centres.

25 April 1981

[A leading article of the same day, headed 'Grand Baby-lon Capsules', commented: 'A niche giving an Osaka businessman ample room to jot down a haiku beside his bonsai tree before retiring might seem cramped to a Wolverhampton representative given to practising golf before the wardrobe mirror, or sprinkling breadcrumbs on the windowsill for the sparrows to find in the morning.'

Slight developments of the technology, including the

introduction of a fork-lift truck, would make it possible to whisk the businessmen to their destinations by air without waking them.]

OLD FOLKS SURVIVE GUN DUEL

CLEVELAND, OHIO   Two old men had a gunfight to settle an old grudge in the hallway of an apartment house here, but all 12 bullets went astray, police said.

With each brandishing an antique pistol, the men – one aged 77 and the other 76 – were standing just five feet apart during the duel. Police theorised that they missed because one needed a cane to prop himself up while firing, and the other had trouble seeing because of glaucoma.

The two men lived in flats opposite each other and began quarrelling in the hallway at about 11 a.m. on Tuesday. They went back into their apartments and came out with the guns, police said. Each fired six shots as a woman walked by.

Residents called police, who took the pair to headquarters. 'There were bullet holes above, bullet holes down, and bullet holes all over the hallway', said one of the detectives.

The men were released after both signed papers saying that they did not wish to press charges against the other, and therefore their names were not released. The 76-year-old man said that they were fighting over a grudge that went back a long way.

Police kept the guns.

8 May 1981

EXPERTS SPLIT ON GAS BOOM THEORY

from Clive Cookson

Occasional booms, sounding like distant artillery or thunder but with no apparent natural or artificial cause, have mystified people in many parts of the world.

They have acquired names like the 'Barisal guns' in the

239

'There were bullet holes all over the hallway . . .'
[OLD FOLKS SURVIVE GUN DUEL]

Ganges delta, 'Mistpoeffers' off the Belgian coast, and 'brontidi' in the Apennine Mountains.

In 1979, two American scientists, Dr Thomas Gold and Dr Steven Soter, of Cornell University, put forward a plausible argument that many of those noises were caused by methane gas escaping from deep in the Earth.

They produced evidence that brontides, the scientific term for unexplained natural booms, were often associated with seismic activity and sometimes preceded big earthquakes.

But in next week's *Science*, Donald Stierman, of the University of California, Riverside, argues against that hypothesis. He believes that enough noise can be generated directly by earth tremors, under certain conditions, to account for brontides, without high pressure gas escaping.

Dr Stierman quotes recent field observations in California of extremely weak earthquakes which generated loud booming noises without any evidence of gas escaping. Large outcrops of bedrock could transmit the sounds from tremors as small as magnitude 1.

He doubts whether high-pressure gas could burst from the Earth, as Dr Gold and Dr Soter describe, without leaving any trace of its eruption. He questions the ability of rocks to hold enough gas under sufficient pressure.

Finally, he picks apart a few of the historical accounts of gas erupting, particularly from mountain sides, and igniting spontaneously, which the Cornell scientists use as supporting evidence.

However, in the same issue of *Science*, Dr Gold and Dr Soter direct a counter-blast at Dr Stierman. They calculate that brontides, 'as loud as nearby thunder', as sometimes reported, would require a ground vibration 10 times greater than the threshold for human detection, and that direct sound generation by an earth tremor could occur only where there were large outcrops of bare rock.

That mechanism could not be responsible for the 'Barisal guns' booming across the alluvial delta of the Ganges.

Dr Gold and Dr Soter dispute Dr Stierman's claim that the release of high-pressure gas would leave a trace. They estimate that a few kilograms of gas at a pressure of several kilobars would make a noise as loud as a stick of dynamite exploding.

If the gas then explodes in the air, ignited by sparks between electrostatically charged dust particles, the sound would be even louder.

Brontides have been reported less frequently in recent times that in past centuries.

10 June 1981

MOREOVER...

by Miles Kington

Thanks to the new technology at The Times, *it has proved possible to merge the Music Research Staff with the Motoring Correspondent, and so become the only paper to road-test the new Yamaha 750 cc Concert Grand.*

Anyone who has ever wondered if a company that specialized in making pianos and building high-powered motor bikes really knew what it was up to will have all his doubts removed when seated at the controls of this remarkable machine.

For years pianists have been complaining of the quality of provincial pianos and prayed for some way of easily transporting a good piano with them; the Yamaha 750 cc Concert Grand is the answer.

Cruising speed is designed to be an easy Allegro Assai, though it can go up to a Vivo or Con Fuoco without any trouble, even if at that tempo the bass response tends to be a little sluggish. I took the Grand on a run from the Wigmore Hall to the Theatre Royal, Bath, in a little less than two hours and could easily have clipped 15 minutes off that time if I had remembered to put the lid down.

Not only did it cruise beautifully but when called upon to negotiate some difficult passages of Chopin on the outskirts of Bath it responded effortlessly.

The most obvious revolutionary feature of the machine is that the driver sits sideways on to the oncoming road. This makes sense for two reasons: it allows for much greater visibility, and it recognizes the fact that pianists feel uneasy if not presenting a profile, though at first it seems a little awkward to look up and see the scenery flash past.

Other drivers seem a little startled as well, and on the way back from Bath I was stopped once or twice by curious policemen. As they were quick to agree, however, there is nothing in motorway regulations to forbid musical instruments being driven on the motorway as long as they are not horsedrawn.*

Comfort is superb throughout. Yamaha has successfully solved the problem of adapting a piano stool to take a safety belt and although passengers are not yet catered for, they are working on a larger model for duets.

I especially like the ashtray which pulls out from under the keyboard, the glove compartment set above the treble register and the illuminated music/map stand; I see no reason why these should not become standard fixtures on all stationary pianos.

Among the innovatory controls are a dual accelerator/loud pedal and a flashing light which comes on if a repeat has not been properly observed. If I have one criticism, it is that the metronome attachment which also serves as a windscreen wiper is slowed by friction with the screen and tends to give inaccurate tempo read-outs.

This revolutionary machine, due on the market in the autumn, comes in three colours: Flaming Scarlatti, Pastoral Brown and Lime Verdi.

18 June 1981

*[But they do not escape the problem of parking. See p.107.]

ROBOTS MAY TAME US YET

Members of Mensa, the international society of highly intelligent persons, were presented yesterday with a vision of a future in which they might be kept as pets by their own robots.

Mr Clive Sinclair, the micro-electronics pioneer and chairman of the British branch of the organization, opened a four-day symposium on science and technology at Queen's College, Cambridge, with a mind-numbing catalogue of predictions.

'A few years ago it took one of the world's largest computers to play a modest game of chess, and now a cheap pocket-size toy can do the same,' he said.

'Each decade brings a 300-fold increase in the complexity available for a given cost or, indeed, size. At that rate machines of economic size will exceed the complexity of the human brain between about AD 2010 and 2020.

'Sadly, whatever we do to enhance our powers we can also do to the robots, or they can do to themselves, and they are likely to be faster thinkers than we are. Perhaps they will be kind enough to keep us as pets.'

23 July 1981

ACKNOWLEDGEMENTS

Thanks are due to the news agencies listed below for permission to include the articles listed:

Permission to reproduce any of these articles except for purposes of comment or review is needed from the relevant news agency as well as from *The Times*.

Stephen Winkworth would like to express his thanks to Miss Patricia Moynagh and to the staff of the London Library, the St Pancras Library and the Central Reference Library for their help.

INDEX OF HEADLINES

INDEX OF TOPICS